Fantasy or Reality?

Peter Moyes

How to replace the Black Hole
of management theory
with the bottom-line benefits of
pragmatism and common sense

Fantasy or Reality?

Fantasy or Reality?

Dedicated to my dearest wife Valerie

This first world edition published 2016 by:

Create Space Publishing Services

Copyright © 2016 by Peter Moyes

A CIP catalogue for this book is available from the British Library:
(Moyes, Peter – Fantasy or Reality?)

ISBN-13:978-1523831814/ISBN-10:1523831812

Typesetting (Book Antiqua) and cover design by Tony Corbin.

My Thanks

So many I have worked for, or with, have directly or indirectly contributed to this book that I cannot even begin to thank them all by name.

I would, however, like to express and record my profound gratitude and thanks to them. In my career I have learned so much from so many and have been helped more than I deserve by many kind colleagues, friends and acquaintances.

One person, who I must name but cannot even begin to adequately thank, is Tony Corbin a colleague and now friend from Digital for his editing, encouragement, help, infinite patience, inspiration and spell checking. The book would never have seen the light of day without his persistence, persuasion and professionalism. I count myself singularly fortunate for his help and have learned so much from him.

The other person I must name is Professor John Black for his superb and professional final edit and penetrating comments. John was my mentor and economics tutor at Oxford and his contribution adds further to his kindness and help that I can never adequately repay.

I have also learned from my grandson Hector who from an early age displayed amazing skills in managing his irascible and unmanageable granddad.

I am, of course, entirely responsible for the contents and particularly for anything a reader may disagree with.

Peter Moyes

Peter Moyes

ABOUT THE AUTHOR

Peter Moyes is long in experience and young in mind with a passion for incisive clarity and elegant simplicity. Much of his sparkle is evident in this book. He was educated first in the university of life, then at Ruskin College and then at the University of Oxford at Merton College as a 29-year-old mature student.

Peter has experienced management at all levels from apprentice to director. He has worked in companies varying in size from 3 employees to multinationals with over 100,000 staff. His management career began at Philips in production where he was, uniquely, the only arts graduate in Philips to become a senior technical manager.

At Multitone he was Technical Director responsible for two factories in the UK, one in Malaysia and design groups in Canada and the UK. Peter also has experience as a non-executive director of Data Recording Instruments Ltd and United Peripherals Ltd.

At Digital Equipment, Peter was a senior management consultant advising corporate customers. He was one of Digital's leading speakers in Europe with a reputation for informed, original and stimulating presentations. He has also enthused and trained Digital consultants in Europe, Hong Kong, Japan, Taiwan, UK and USA.

Fantasy or Reality?

Contents

Fantasy or Reality?

Introduction

The spectre of theory haunts management. There has always been a gap between theory and practice. There is now a black hole of fantasy models, techniques and theories confronting management. What managerial leaders do in the confused, imperfect and uncertain world of management differs vastly from what the academics, in their theoretical, idealised and utopian world, say managers should do.

Tellingly, the theory-practice gap is even prevalent within academic institutions. A long time ago, I taught management techniques and theories at my local College of Further Education to part-time students, studying for a diploma in management. The Management Studies Department propagated management theories as an academic discipline. Yet its own management and organisation was poor and its practices were far removed from its theories, as indeed was the wider management of the college.

The Catering Department for instance taught its students how to prepare superb food, yet the food, hygiene and service in the college canteen was appalling. It was as if there was an invisible wall separating what the teaching part of the college *taught* from what the administrative part of the college *did*.

What the syllabus said I was supposed to teach and what the books said bore little resemblance to how my managerial colleagues and I actually managed. This caused some embarrassment since some of the students worked for me. Also because I taught up to 20 techniques and only ever used one or two them myself, I had to be a little economical with the truth. I explained, tongue-in-cheek, that they had to understand most of them to:

a) Pass their exams (which was true)
b) Develop their knowledge and thinking skills (which, at best, was partly true).

Almost all my students passed the externally adjudicated examinations (some secured distinctions) but in truth, I doubt whether the course did them much practical good. Learning about management techniques the experts say managers *should* use but *don't* is hardly sensible.

With the exponential growth in management theories and techniques the gap between theory and practice has now become a creativity-thwarting chasm. Theories have multiplied and managers are now so beset with gobbledygook, management babble, models, techniques and theories that there is an epidemic of that most disabling and painful of all managerial diseases - paralysis by analysis. There is simply no way managers can sort the wheat from the chaff, absorb more than a fraction of the theories or do anything about an even smaller fraction of them even if they were so foolish as to want to do so.

The spread of theory is now so pervasive that we have reached the absurd situation where some managers in large corporations employ consultants and others simply to think for them. They spend small fortunes on obtaining advice they mostly ignore. This is probably just as well because many who follow 'by the book' advice from consultants often end up in chaos! There are managers so steeped in management theories that they are incapable of doing anything without the blessing of a consultant or guru. The shelf life of some management theories is now often so short that they are obsolete almost as soon as they are propagated.

A case in point is with so-called strategic thinking or strategic intent. An erudite Harvard professor[i] has identified 85 strategy frameworks that the Management Myth Making Industry has offered to prospective clients over the years. They range from *Ansoff Matrix* to *Transient Competitive Advantage*. The strategy gurus seem to operate on the principle of making the simple highly complex. For me a strategy is a description of where an organisation wants to be in the future and what it is going to do to get there. It is hard to see how using a fancy framework of high-powered jargon makes formulating a strategy easier.

The growth of management consultancy is equally pervasive and is a cause and consequence of the explosion of theories. Management consultancy companies have been enjoying an "anything for a quick buck"[ii] feeding frenzy. In 2009-10, the British Government spent over £1bn

---

[i] *Panka J Ghemawat Competition and business strategy in historical perspective. Business history review, 2002 - Cambridge University Press*

[ii] *David Craig – Rip-Off! The scandalous inside story of the management consultancy money machine.*
(The original Book Company) ISBN 1-872188-06-0

on management consultancy and interim managers. No wonder UK government so often seems such a manager-less and mindless shambles.

By 2013, according to the Management Consulting Association (MCA) the overall spend on management consultancy in the UK had risen to £4.8 billion. Meantime, consultant numbers totalled 35,000 - an increase of 16% on the previous year.

Most of these mega-expensive consultancy studies end up gathering dust and/or clogging up so-called knowledge databases.

It is, of course, true that theory has an important role in managerial leadership but not one where it literally enslaves and dominates management as it does now. This book is therefore about:

- Swinging the pendulum from theory back to reality.
- Calling a spade a spade.
- Challenging the conventional wisdom of modern management theory.
- Advocating, as an antidote to management by theory, an unfashionable common sense and pragmatic approach to managerial leadership.
- Using managerial leadership, as distinct from administrative management, at *all* levels of an organisation.
- Casting out theories from fantasy land.

Hopefully the evidence, analyses, ideas and judgements contained here, accumulated from over 40 years' experience, will provide confidence and solace to those managers who distrust the surfeit of theoretical explanations and techniques that now beset management.

Hopefully, too, it will resonate for those whose managerial skills are grounded in experience gained at the sharp-end of management who share my doubts and scepticism about the unhealthy dependence on the drug of management theory.

This book is a manifesto for removing that dependency and the black hole it has created. It tells the story about what is wrong with the theories and how to put things right in practice.

Introduction

PART ONE: *FANTASY*

Just What Has Gone Wrong?

Fantasy or Reality?

Chapter 1 - Theoretical Gobbledygook

One of the greatest tragedies of life is the murder of a beautiful theory by a gang of brutal facts – *BENJAMIN FRANKLIN*

Our imaginative skills and our abilities to think in abstract terms are astonishing and almost certainly beyond our practical understanding. This is strength and a weakness. There is seemingly no limit to our individual and collective intellectual abilities to imagine, conceptualise and create - *the* defining characteristics of Homo sapiens. As the Russian novelist Fyodor Dostoevsky put it: '… men love abstract reasoning and neat systematisation so much that they think nothing of distorting the truth, closing their eyes and ears to contrary evidence to preserve their logical constructions'.[i]

This is certainly true of management theories that are too often gobbledygook and very often distort the truth. It is difficult to sort the wheat from the chaff in management theories where the chaff exceeds the wheat by such a large margin. The dilemma is that while we cannot manage without theoretical insights it is frequently difficult if not impossible to manage with the mountain of theory that confronts modern management.

We have become submerged by the exponential growth of management theory and the claims of the soothsayers who propagate them. What ultimately matters in management

---

[i] Fydor Dostovsky *Notes from the Underground* (Kindle edition)

is how we use our theories, insights and skills to make a beneficial difference. Knowledge, theories, skills and genius are only of value if they are used effectively. Otherwise they are empty and devoid of the achievement, meaning or the purpose that is the very essence of management.

Theories are, of course, only ever a partial analysis and incomplete explanation because no one who is inside and part of a system can ever fully understand it. A deaf mouse nesting in a grand piano has no means of knowing it has done so. Only someone outside the mouse-grand piano system can do so. We are all mouse like in seeking insight and understanding via theories.

In the first part of the 20th century, scientists perceived the universe with a Newtonian certainty. They mostly believed they had an accurate and stable picture of the eternal scientific truths of the physical world. These beliefs were subsequently shattered with the advent of Einstein's special theory of relativity, Heisenberg's uncertainty principle, the emergence of the complex conundrum of quantum physics and Popper's falsification principle.

Scientists, unlike some management theorists, now know they do not know and cannot know with any degree of certainty or finality. They can continually extend the boundaries of knowledge but never get there. The final nail in the coffin of scientific certainly came when Godal showed in 1931 that Russell and Whitehead were wrong to claim in their seminal work *Principia Mathematica* that mathematics is both consistent and correct. If mathematics is not certain how can any other theory ever be so? As Karl Popper[ii] pointed out even scientific theories can never qualify as an ultimate truth because they can only be *disproved* never *proved*. If a scientific theory predicts there will be an eclipse at a specific date, time and location this can be verified by empirical observation but this does not prove the theory is a timeless, immutable and eternal truth.

The irony is that while scientific thinkers have moved away from certainties, many management thinkers tend to hype management theories as immutable, Newtonian-like truths and try to sell them like washing powder. My theory or technique washes whiter than yours. They are based on the erroneous assumption that the scientific methods used so successfully for the study of sciences are applicable to the study of management and social phenomena. This is absolutely not appropriate.

In extreme situations management theories are built on pseudo-scientific foundations even down to the use of absurd pseudo algebraic equations or pseudo set theory such as this one (overleaf) used to describe/explain a matrix organisation[iii]:

[ii] Bryan Magee *Popper* (London: Fontana/Collins). June 1976. ISBN 0 00 632993 4. p. 38-40.
[iii] Robert G Eccles and Nitin Nohria with James D Berkley *Beyond the Hype* (Harvard Business School) ISBN 0-87584-506-1. p. 129. The table apparently originated from Stanley M Davis and Paul R Lawrence *Matrix* (Reading, Mass Addison-Wesley) 1977.

Matrix Organisation	Matrix Structure	Matrix Systems	Matrix Culture	Matrix Behaviour
=	+	+	+	+

Readers can make of this what they will. My inclination is to suggest that someone should create a Golden Gobbledygook Award to complement the Golden Fleece Award mentioned in chapter 6!

The reality is that all managerial and social theories and models are suspect. At best they are only a crude approximation of reality. At worst they are one sided or wholly misleading. An Economist's theory of management is different to an Anthropologist's, Chemist's, Engineer's, Historian's, Philosopher's, Physicist's, Psychologist's, Poet's or Sociologist's etc. This is necessarily so because different academic disciplines bring different insights and perceptions. There is no objective or scientific way of knowing whether any are right or wrong. Non-scientific theories are always circular, self-referential and shaped and influenced by their proponent's background, the questions they ask and the metaphors they use.

At the end of the day we are all prisoners of, and limited by, language and logic in our intellectual and managerial endeavours and in the expression and understanding of our concepts and theories. Unfortunately, language is a quagmire and logic is a surprisingly frail tool. One day a bright child asked a Priest "Father, can God do anything?" The Priest replied, "Yes my child". The child thought and then asked "Father if God can do everything, can He make something so large and heavy that God cannot lift it?" This story, told by Edward de Bono, in one of his many stimulating books, clearly illustrates the limitations of logic and language and why we need to be much more cautious about uncritically accepting managerial and social theories.

Some scientific theories can overcome the problems caused by the inherent limitation of the language of words by using the language of mathematics to aid insight, understanding and explanation. This route however is not open to management theories. Also many scientific theories result from experimental methods, which can be confirmed by repeating the experiment. Again no such route is available for management theories so their standard of verification is much, much lower than scientific theories and mostly non-existent.

This means the scope for charlatans, wishful thinking and whistling in the wind is enormous. Almost any mad idea can be dressed up as a theory and alas too many are as will become evident later in this book.

A further problem with theories, particularly non-scientific ones, is the explicit and implicit assumptions they are built upon. For instance a large part of economic theory was for decades build upon three suspect premises[iv]:

1. Human beings are rational in their buying choices – this is not true.

[iv] David Orrell *Economy the Ten Ways That Economics Get it Wrong* (Kindle edition)

2. Choices are made autonomously irrespective of the influence of other consumers - again not true.
3. Feedback loops – negative or positive – did not exist in the market place whereas they obviously do.

The result was that while Economists were propounding the benefits of competition and market forces, Business Schools were busy devising means whereby companies could avoid price competition by brand management and other means to create in effect quasi monopolies.

Additionally, the so-called research underpinning management theories may be based on unproven theories or premises creating, what in impolite circles is sometimes called "a buggers muddle ".

We use theories, models and hypotheses to extend and explain the boundaries of knowledge and understanding, to gain insights and to test conjectures. They are an essential part of our mental processes. Management theories are too often misused, in some cases almost to the point where if the facts don't fit the theories, the facts must be wrong. The ultimate absurdity was when a French management team I read about became concerned because they feared that something that worked in practice would not do so in theory! Instead of providing the practical understanding manager's need they are assailed by complex intellectual fantasies or edifices of the kind Dostoevsky describes.

This also happens when theories become prescriptive instead of descriptive such as when a theory is used to promote a particular management technique or techniques. The classic example was when attempts were made to transform management into a science and create the myth of scientific management. It is amazing how many were and are intellectually seduced by such tosh. Regrettably some still are.

Managers don't and can't live purely in a world of conjecture and theory. They live in the practical world of uncertainty, ambiguity, action and results. Some theories *may* help them to understand their practical world but far too many create confusion instead of crystal clear clarity. What ultimately matters in management is how we use our theories, insights and skills to make a beneficial difference. Knowledge, theories, skills and genius are only of value if they are used effectively. Otherwise they are empty and devoid of the achievement, meaning or the purpose that is the essence of management.

Many of the hypotheses about management are meaningless and some are more rhetorical than intellectual. One academic claimed 'Managers find themselves in the uncomfortable and discomforting world of chaos and complexity theory. There is much talk of fractals and cognitive dissonance. Uncertainty and ambiguity are the new realities'.

All this is news to me and I suspect to most managers. The truth is that there are no 'new realities' in management of the sort described. Management has always been chaotic and complex. That is why managers are needed. Management has always been 'uncomfortable and discomforting'. Managers have always had to cope with uncertainty and ambiguity. They all come with the territory.

There is not a shred of evidence to suggest that managers are kept awake at night worrying about chaos and complexity theories or that when they go to sleep they dream about using fractals to boost sales. These are scientific hypotheses about the nature of the universe not the day-to-day concerns of practical managers and have no relevance to the day-to-day practice of management. As to 'cognitive dissonance'[v], the typical manager is probably not even sure what it means. I certainly didn't. I am not sure I do even now and no manager has ever talked to me about it.

This does not mean managers are philistines or that they have tunnel vision. They are often highly intelligent and prescient with a keen interest in the world around them. They want to know what is happening, what is changing and how it affects their enterprise or organisation. Many have a scientific bent. But few practical managers buy the rhetoric, which is now so commonplace in the

[v] According to my dictionary "cognitive" means "capable of cognition" (i.e. "knowledge: apprehension: knowing in the widest sense") and "dissonance" means "want of harmony" so "cognitive dissonance" presumably means something like "knowledge without harmony" or "knowing without harmony". Presumably that means something profound to someone.

Management Myth Making Industry. A diet of 'core competencies', 'transcendental solutions', 'strategic intent', 'disintermediation', 'high velocity management' or whatever happens to be the buzzwords of management babble, soon begin to pall when there are *real* issues and problems which need attention.

There is a further serious weakness of management and social theories. It is that they rarely, if ever, explicitly state where the theory or model is supposed to work and where it will fail. In 1936 John Maynard Keynes published *The General Theory of Employment of Interest and Money* but did not specify any boundary conditions. What may work well in an industrial economy may not work in a post-industrial economy of the information age. Such an economy is quite foreign to Keynes' experience and thinking.

Management and social theories are two sided. If we cannot manage with theories we clearly cannot manage without them either. Theories provide frameworks. The issue is not a black and white one of theory versus no theory. The dilemma facing all practical managers is how to use common sense (itself an abstract and subjective concept) to cope with the theories and the paradoxes that are an integral part of management (and life).

Managers don't have to be told '...complex adaptive systems are composed of a diversity of agents that interact with each other, mutually affect each other and in so doing, generate behaviour for the system as a whole, such as in evolution, ecosystems and the human mind'?[vi] The captain of the Titanic would hardly have been grateful to be appraised of this insight during the panic-stricken four hours that his ship was sinking! It reminds me of a supposedly seminal article on economics, I read in my undergraduate days. It was entitled 'Everything is related but some things are more related than others'. Well, er, yes!

Napoleon believed there was nothing theoretical about war. You do what you have to do and do it fast. There is nothing theoretical either about management. Good managers make haste slowly in thinking about what should be done but then make haste quickly in doing it.

Management theory is unfortunately increasingly about minutiae, which can have no possible interest to the practicing manager for whom life is already far too short. I had lunch one day with the Head of the Management School at a British University. He had a refreshingly practical and common sense approach to management, unusual in academia, probably because he had a hands-on management background. Yet his conversation was liberally sprinkled with references to the latest management research.

The difference between management by the book and practical management is in some ways reflected in the differences between the approach of Aristotle and Galileo. Aristotle *theorised* that heavy objects would fall faster than light objects. Galileo *proved* by practical experiments that

---

[vi] Roger Lewin and Birute Regine *The Soul of Work*

heavy and light objects fall at the same speed. He then had the misfortune to be hauled before the Inquisition because his views challenged Aristotelian conventional wisdom. In oversimplified terms, Managers are the heirs of Galileo, Management Theorists the heirs of Aristotle.

There has always been a gap between theory and practice and presumably always will be. Within reason that is not a problem. Practical managers, who are used to dilemmas and paradoxes, can live with that. What they cannot live with is a situation where theory runs wild and overrides the dictates of common sense, experience and wisdom as it now too often does.

The study of management has alas become like the study of literature. One perceptive commentator described this as:

> *'bloated with hangers-on: doctors of literature, devotees of specific writers, advocates of particular literary styles, chroniclers of literary gossip, perpetual secretaries of literary organisations, linguists, and literary historians to name just a few. Once the main subjects had been analysed the next generation of literary doctors had to focus on smaller and smaller details. They spent decades giving meaning to the tiniest aspects of each writers life and then snarled at each other over the corpse.'*[vii]

By 2002 there were apparently a staggering 400

[vii] John Raulson Saul *Voltaire's Bastards* (New York: Vintage Books) 1993. ISBN 0-697-78419-9. P 555

biographies about Lord Byron in existence. He must surely be the ultimate juicy literary corpse – *the* corpse of corpses - for them to snarl over! There is, as yet, no equivalent corpse in management studies thank goodness and management theory has not yet reached such a degree of sterility although it is clearly heading that way.

There are more teachers and students of literature than they are writers. The literary professionals have such things as long-term contracts, university tenure and pension plans. The writers, on whom they feed, are usually either at the bottom of the food chain and the pecking order or dead (preferable as they can't answer back). In some traditional universities, not that long ago, you could not research authors who were still alive. The few rich writers, who cater for a mass market, are often looked upon with disdain by the literary establishment because they don't write like Dickens, Shakespeare or Trollope. There are, of course, notable exceptions such as J K Rowling and J R Tolkien, whose books are a fertile feeding ground for academic study and speculation and are likely to be so for very many years to come and even perhaps posthumously promoted to the status of literary corpse.

The ratio of theorisers to doers in management is probably less than in literature but there are almost certainly more people theorising about management, teaching management studies and consulting about managers than there are managers. According to Wikipedia in 2009 the consultancy industry worldwide had a turnover of $300 billion. According to Chris Woodhead[viii] there were a staggering 7,476[ix] management courses and 5,816 business ones offered by Universities in the UK in 2002. The US apparently trains 80,000 MBA's a year. The mind boggles. How to goodness can management become any better when so many are trained in so much suspect theory?

Fortunately not much use is apparently made of MBA indoctrination. One study found that 73% of those with MBAs were 'used only marginally or not at all in their first managerial assignments'. Research suggests that 'little of what is taught in colleges or even business schools really prepares would-be managers for the realities of management.'[x] It is, perhaps, just as well because, according to Peter Drucker, 'The business schools in the U.S., set up less than a century ago, have been preparing well trained clerks …'[xi] John Ralston Saul with some truth defined Business Schools as 'Acting schools which train experts in abstract management methods to pretend they are capitalists'[xii]!

There is, of course, a crucial difference between the study

[viii] Former controversial Chief Inspector of Ofsted the body charged with reporting on school standards and performance in the UK.
[ix] Estimates of this kind need to be taken with a large pinch of salt. It would not surprise me if the real figure was twice as large or half as much. Those who produce such estimates can come up with almost any figure because no one knows what the truth is and no one can challenge them.
[x] Internet: Blurb Buddies - "Fast Companies". December 1998
[xi] Peter F Drucker The Age of Discontinuity (William Heinman: London 1969) ISBN 0 330 02693 3 p 372
[xii] John Ralston Saul The Doubter's Companion (Free Press, New York ISBN 0-02-927722-1)

of literature and the study of management. The study of literature has no direct practical impact on what happens in the world, whereas the study of management does. The study of literature is essentially a cerebral activity examining the nature and purpose of life. The study of management is about, or should be about, how to translate ideas in the mind into reality in the world. Yet the theorists continue to apply the same academic approach (they usually call it a methodology) to the study of management as is used for literature and similar social studies.

As a result, management studies too often promote the illusion of theory and the Management Myth Making Industry has almost as much influence as medieval theology used to have. One writer on management, Stephen Pattison, who has a background in theology and public services, believes management theory is the great unacknowledged religious faith of the late 20th century. He believes 'the sooner we acknowledge it, the better for all our business and public services.'[xiii] Personally I very much doubt this but it is an interesting thought.

There is not yet an inquisition as such in management but there are certainly enormous subtle pressures within management for political correctness. This even extends to the use and abuse of language and in the European Union; it is increasingly embodied in legislation. It is called killing the goose that lays the golden egg. The business schools teach a particular (or peculiar?) kind of thinking which is akin to indoctrination. Anyone who has the temerity to

---

[xiii] Stephen Pattison *The Faith of the Managers*

write a book like this one is hardly likely to find executive placement consultants beating a path to their door. Fortunately I am not waiting for them to do so!!

Part of the appeal, of the Management Myth Making Industry, lies in its jargon. It is rich in evocative, memorable and titillating words and phrases many of which, on examination, prove to be sheer unadulterated nonsense. These include 'boundaryless' companies, 'computerless' computer companies, customer care, cycle time compression, chaos theory, dancing elephants, empty rain coats, excellence, liberation management, methodologies, nanosecond management, paradigm shifts, re-engineering, thinking horizontally rather than vertically, situational leadership, turbulence, virtual organisations and so on. The list is endless, ever changing and alas, growing at an alarming rate.

One of the most disturbing aspects is how the theory industry distorts and inflates language in the name of clarity and progress. According to a sales leaflet distributed by Compaq in the UK we don't have suppliers any more, we have 'Channel Partners'. This is, of course, simply marketing hype. There are only ever customers and suppliers. A supplier buys Compaq computers from the manufacturer and sells to their customer or there may be more than one buy-sell link in the chain from manufacturer to end-user. Because some of the links co-operate (and they would be foolish if they didn't) does not make them partners in the normal meaning of the word. The growth of double speak in management is equally alarming. A Microsoft spokesman, asked about the future of a product, explained, 'We're sort of in the Hegelian synthesis of figuring out where the products go once they've encountered the reality of the marketplace.' In other words Microsoft had a duff product no one wanted. Why didn't he say so? Goodness knows what Hegel had to do with it. Somehow I don't think that my former political theory tutor Dr Zbigniew Pelczynski[xiv], a Hegelian Scholar, would regard the Microsoft explanation of a Hegelian synthesis as accurate!

Buzzwords and acronyms, particularly three letter abbreviations (TLA's), abound and have increased apace with the growth in management theories. They are now so common that one computer company has found it necessary to add FLA's (four letter abbreviations) to their TLA database when they ran out of three letter ones. Dr Johnson said 'Language is the dress of thought'. In management it has become fancy dress. What truth buzzword and acronyms are supposed to illuminate is anybody's guess. There is certainly no shortage of them.

We have 'autonomous management', 'commitment based management' and 'team based management' plus countless other kinds and varieties. We have 'strategic intent' and 'strategic alliances'. The management theorists seem to have an insatiable compulsion to titillate the mind. According to a McKinsey training film, 'to be lean is to be liberated'. What ever will they dream up next? In the meantime, just ponder what we already have to endure!

[xiv] For many years a fellow of Pembroke College, Oxford

The buzzwords of illusion

SYNERGY	BRAND VALUE	GAP ANALYSIS	BEST PRACTICE	BOTTOM LINE	EMPOWER
REVISIT	THINKING OUTSIDE THE BOX	HARDBALL	BENCH MARK	CORE BUSINESS	LEVEL PLAYING FIELD
VALUE ADDED	PROACTIVE	WIN-WIN	BIG PICTURE	FAST TRACK	MARKET DRIVEN
RESULT DRIVEN	PUSHING THE ENVELOPE	KNOWLEDGE BASE	TOTAL QUALITY	TOUCH BASE	TIME FRAME
MINDSET	CLIENT FOCUSSED	BALL PARK	GAME PLAN	LEVERAGE	CUTTING EDGE
NO BRAINER	STRATEGIC FIT	WINDOW OF OPPORTUNITY	DRILL DOWN	LEFT FIELD	OUT OF THE LOOP
DISINTER-MEDIATION	GEOMGETIC MODELLING	EXPONENTIAL SMOOTHING	MARKETIN G LED	BURN RATE	HIGH PERFORMANCE WORK SYSTEMS
BORAD CANVASS	BUE SKY THINKING	BALANCED SCRORECARD	VIRTUAL ORGANISA TION	LEARNING ORGANISATI ON	CHAOS THEORY
PARADIGM SHIFT	CORE COMPETENCIE S	PUSH THE ENVELOPE	STEP UP TO THE PLATE	GOING FORWARD	ON THE RADAR

There are now even PowerPoint templates for propagating the illusions available on the Internet. One vendor offers an incredible 15,000. I examined a few of them and thought the content mainly gibberish although some of the slides were pretty. Others were complex and confusing.

Management theories are ten a penny, which is more than most of them, are worth. They generate a huge volume of froth and obscure true knowledge and wisdom. Management mythmakers produce the froth. They put raw hype and gobbledygook in and get pure hype out.

The mythmakers create more confusion than clarity. As Ian MacLaurin, who led Tesco to supermarket leadership in the UK put it: 'I have no intention of joining those gurus who spin their theories of 'transaction processing' and 'geometric modelling', of TQM (Total Quality Management) and ES (Exponential Smoothing). They only succeed in making a mystery of the subject. The world is already complex enough, without having to make a secret of what, so often, is a matter of common sense.'[xv] Good for him.

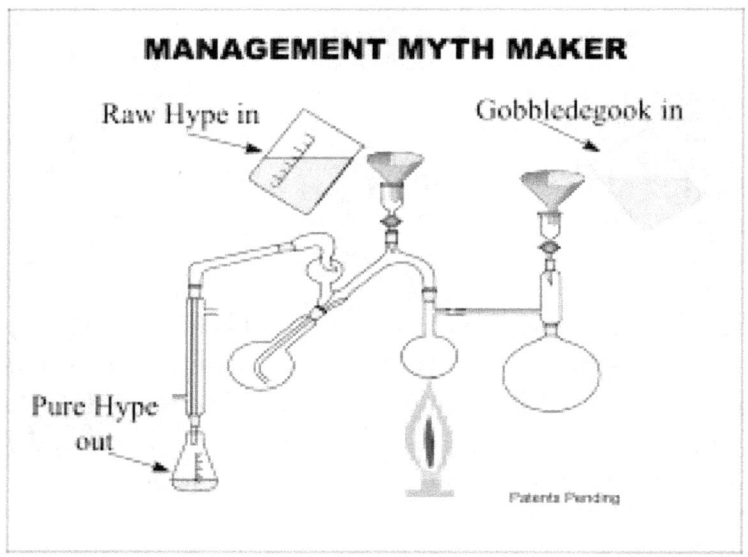

A friend with leftward leanings, Jack Lerner, once told me there should be more state planning because planning was the reason for the success of large multinationals. He would change his mind if he saw how appalling planning and management is in large, bureaucratic multinational corporations and the extent to which Comrade Lenin's first disastrous five-year plan relied heavily on the "expertise" of US "experts" in scientific management. St Luke asked 'which of you intending to build a tower sitteth not down

[xv] Ian MacLaurin *Tiger by the Tail* (Pan Books: London) ISBN 0 330 37371 4 p11

first and counteth the cost?' The answer is too often "Not many".

One perceptive Japanese commentator claimed way back in 1982 that many large multinational organisations were 'run like the Soviet economy'. He quoted a Japanese planner who said the strategic planning process looked as complicated as building a chemical plant.[xvi] Where is the sense in that?

The pendulum in management has clearly swung too far and effective managerial leadership is in real danger of being obliterated by theorists and theories with their emphasis on management by administration, bureaucracy and theory. The truth is that management where it matters, at the point of impact, has to be simple, clear and practical if it is to succeed. It is now far too often complex, confused and impracticable.

We need to redress the balance, emphasise the need for common sense, re-ground management in the leadership, organisation and motivation of people instead of in the pursuit of theory. Managers will then be able to do what they are supposed to do: improve the lot of human kind by providing the kind of managerial leadership that makes a beneficial difference.

The pragmatic approach to management, advocated in

[xvi] Kenichi Ohmae *The Mind of the Strategist* (MacGraw-Hill: New York 1982). ISBN 0-07-047595-4 p 224

this book, is therefore to explicitly recognise that management:

1. Is not a purely or primarily a cerebral activity and there are limits to what we can do in management with the intellect alone;
2. Is ultimately about what *actually* happens in practice not what *should* happen in theory. Managers have to get up and go. They can't sit down and theorise until the cows come home;
3. Has to use the more practical levels of the intellect including experience, intuition and wisdom;
4. Theory is only one of the many dimensions in the managerial equation and all management theories are subjective not objective;
5. Is itself as much subjective as objective;
6. At an intellectual level is primarily a process of synthesis and not one of analysis;
7. Whatever we do we will always consciously or sub-consciously run up against insoluble paradoxes and excruciating dilemmas;
8. Came first whilst theories and techniques came second. Human beings have managed rather well for centuries without any management textbooks, theories or business schools.
9. Has to cope with organisational and other complexities we cannot possibly hope to understand. (If that worries the reader then remember this is also true of life, only more so.)

Then all successful managers already know all this don't

they?

Fantasy or Reality?

CHAPTER 2 - Utopian Illusions

... the utopian approach must lead to a dangerous dogmatic attachment to a blueprint for which countless sacrifices have been made.
— KARL POPPER

Most of us, even hardened cynics like me, have a utopian view of management and organisations. The idealism inherent in human nature inclines us, consciously or unconsciously, to believe companies and organisations can be designed, built and managed so that they run like clockwork, with surgical precision and in near perfect harmony. This is in spite of all the substantial evidence to the contrary and in spite of common sense.

The quest for perfection is rooted deep in the human psyche. Virtually all modern theories of management, much endeavour in management and the vast majority of the huge number of articles and books about management are based, implicitly or explicitly, on a utopian, mechanistic and intellectual ideal of management. Who wants a confused and messy reality when they can have a nice, neat, pretend fantasy theory?

Utopia is, of course, an imaginary state – utopia means nowhere or no-place. The concept may date back as far as 1940 BC and utopian theories have always had a powerful hold over the human mind. They have an inner consistency, an intellectual symmetry and a life and mental fascination all of their own. When viewing the world from within the intellectual confines of their seductive and reductionist logic, it is all too easy to forget that all models and theories are abstractions of reality and provide only a partial and therefore distorted view of the world. Theories are necessarily partial because this is the only way we can cope with a complexity we cannot understand. They almost always use highly suspect analogies or metaphors and are often hopelessly impracticable.

Utopian theories are what business schools teach. They are illusions that theorists' harbour; they are ideals that idealists cherish; and they are also, alas, tools that tyrants use. Five of the most evil men of the twentieth century — Hitler, Lenin, Mao, Pol Pot and Stalin — propagated utopian belief systems and blueprints as a tool for repression and tyranny. Some intellectuals outside their countries actually believed in and defended the tyrants because of the deceptively compelling logic of their theories. Intelligence is no proof against mistaken beliefs. Highly intelligent people are frequently the more gullible and dogmatic, presumably because they are seduced by the seemingly elegant logic inherent in all belief systems.

When obsessive management belief systems become utopian they are as much a threat to 'open management' as political belief systems are to the Open Society The consequences of management belief systems, while often harmful, are, of course, much less harmful than political belief systems. Killing people is never part of a manager's job description — unless that is – they are military planners or are an integral part of some highly illegal activity.

One utopian management belief system, popular in the late 1960's and early 1970's, was Management by Objectives (MBO) first expounded as a theory by Peter Drucker in his seminal work *The Practice of Management*. Some years later John Humble in the UK made a praiseworthy and valiant attempt to devise a means of translating the principles of MBO into practice. The basis was ostensibly logical and sensible. Set objectives for an organisation and the individuals in it and link the objectives at one level to those at the next level.

In practice, MBO was mostly an expensive and bureaucratic failure although it did earn a lot of money for consultants advising organisations on attempts to implement MBO. There was literally, at one time, a mini-industry devoted to Management by Objectives. Its influence was so great that some of the Industrial Training Boards in the UK (set up by misguided politicians who hadn't a clue what management was about) made its use mandatory for companies who applied for a rebate of their training levy. The bureaucrats in the training boards loved it - it was Stalinism without the gulags. Those of us, who thought it nonsense, as I did, pretended to implement it just to get some of our own money back.

The carrots used by the industrial training boards to induce companies to use MBO were so complex and unwieldy that in MEL Equipment Co Ltd., we actually wrote a computer programme for Les Todd, the training manager, to calculate how Philips as a whole in the UK should fill in the forms to maximise the value of the rebate.

That one simple programme, written in BASIC and run on a time-shared computer system using a telex terminal, saved a tidy sum for Philips Industries. We did not cheat, we simply used a computer to work out the best combination to maximise refunds.

The generalisations of Management Utopianism are frequently based on unsubstantiated and anecdotal stories of companies, organisations and leaders who are perceived to be outstandingly successful. Yet truly outstanding successes are often the unsung ones. The achievement of a managerial leader who saves his or her company in a hostile environment is often much greater than a management who, say, doubles growth and profits in an expanding market. Winston Churchill regarded success as 'the ability to go from failure to failure without losing your enthusiasm' - a precept I would commend to all managers. As Confucius put it: 'Our greatest glory is not in never failing, but in rising every time we fail.'

The utopians love to construct theories around what outstanding leaders achieve and how the theorists believed they do so. Beware however, utopians are fickle and are forever changing their role, modus operandi and their minds. The fame of the heroic leaders, who are selected as role models for management theorists, is short lived. Those elevated to the pantheon of leadership exemplars don't stay there long. For most, their fame is ephemeral and transient. Management heroes of today are the management failures of tomorrow (sorry about that Mr. Gates!). Management utopianism thrives on ever changing fashions in role models as well as theories.

Analysis of what makes for success is translated by the utopians into simplistic formulas to provide a cook book approach to management. A seven-step approach seems to be a good seller and a mosaic of ideas, observations and rules of thumb also seems to sell well. To prove their formulae are correct, the high priests of Management Utopia use anecdotal evidence and war stories. They infer that success will be assured by following their cookbook formulae. Management utopians also love the grand design, the all-embracing theory of everything.

The language of utopianism is an ever-variable feast. Words mean what the utopians say they mean as they did in *Alice in Wonderland*. We don't change companies anymore, we re-engineer them. People are not made redundant; they are 'right sized'. Losses are simply 'negative profits'. The gobbledygook has to be seen to be disbelieved. The King has no clothes on but no one dares tell the utopian gurus and theoreticians. Whatever happened to old-fashioned common sense and plain language?

They hype promoting Knowledge Management, for example, really is mind numbing. According to the upmarket consultancy, Bain & Company, Knowledge Management requires managers to:
- *Catalogue and evaluate the organisation's current knowledge base;*
- *Determine which competencies will be key to future*

success and what base of knowledge is needed to build a
sustainable leadership position therein;

- *Invest in systems and processes to accelerate the accumulation of knowledge;*
- *Assess the impact of such systems on leadership, culture, and hiring practices;*
- *Codify new knowledge and turn it into tools and information that will improve both product innovation and profitability*

Whew! In all conscience it is hard to see how any practical manager with an atom of sense, or a modicum of experience, could take this seriously. Next thing they'll be talking about will be "Wisdom Management". Heaven forbid!

The reality is that Knowledge Management is simply hype for Information Management — organising information in such a way as to make it available to everyone in an enterprise who needs it. No one with any sense would doubt that sharing information widely is a good thing, but anyone with a bit of gumption would be highly sceptical of the more extravagant benefits claimed for Knowledge Management or indeed its practicability.

Why did they misuse the word knowledge instead of using the word information? Probably because hype and spin is everything in Management Utopianism. People make a good living out of new theories and need fancy catch phrases to catch the attention of potential punters. There is nothing new about what they are saying. The holy grail of computer sales people has always been a so-called integrated database where everyone can find everything. But even computer companies have failed to reach this Eldorado. Their own systems are as much of a shambles as their customers and I write from direct experience as a former employee of a computer manufacturer.

The real problem facing management and society, which the knowledge management theorists have not addressed, is the explosive growth in the volume or extra somatic information (i.e. information outside the brain) and the human capacity to handle it within the brain. Thanks to technology, information is accumulating *exponentially* yet knowledge based on learning, experience and the understanding of information is at best growing *incrementally*. Human wisdom, which enables us to use knowledge effectively, appears to grow very slowly - if at all. Information is now independent of time and location but our brains are still firmly stuck in the present. A sobering thought!

The proponents of utopianism are superb salesmen (they are still predominately masculine) often with charismatic and persuasive personalities and strong and sincere convictions. Some 'Masters of the Universe' are larger than life personalities and have a messianic fervour. The have found *the truth* and they proclaim it with a confidence, certainty and verve which often borders on fanaticism. Many of the gurus *and* the gurus' gurus are consummate actors and entertainers who could earn a good living in Hollywood.

Some really are masters of language and rhetoric. I know of one charismatic guru whose rhetoric is brilliant. He engages his audience using Christian names, he shocks them and he is brilliant at contrasting the good and the bad. He is a master of projecting a scenario of imminent doom and then transforming it into a promised land. One of his final perorations is a story about a disabled person who climbs a mountain. This brings tears to the eyes of the audience (and himself) and by an incredible sleight of hand he links this to using computers better! His seminars are like revivalist meetings. No wonder he is able to command astronomic fees. Whether it does much good or not is another matter.

The utopians are always eminently plausible. Their articles, books and seminars describe their answers, models and methodologies in detail with a Marxist fervour and conviction. They are usually well written and enjoyable and stimulating to read. Although critical of many of them, I must confess that I used to be an avid reader of management books and still succumb naively to the temptation to buy and even read and enjoy them now and then. Business Schools embellish and teach the theories with case studies and the like. The gurus bask in academic respectability. Their proof positive is that their practices are based on observations of what World Class Companies - no less - are supposed to do. What could be more compelling or more persuasive (or more circular) than that?

The beliefs and convictions of the utopians, combined with

a human desire for reassurance and a readiness to accept a cookbook approach to management, have fuelled the creation and growth of the Management Myth Making Industry. It is the engine of utopianism. The soothsayers, gurus, experts, advisers, academics, consultants and the like are all, in one way or another, purveyors of assertions, beliefs, dogma, ex cathedra pronouncements, immutable truths, and managerial mysticism.

The utopian leviathans have grown so much in influence and size that many practicing managers are thoroughly bemused and hardly know what to believe or do. The sheer volume of advice, theories and cookbooks is intimidating. Some so-called managers are so mesmerised by the surfeit of utopian theories that they never do anything unless a consultant or 'expert' is on hand to advise them. They even employ people to think for them in so-called 'think tanks'. The 'experts' and 'thinkers' usually turn out to have very expensive feet of clay and profess to know almost everything but too often understand nothing.

The answers offered by the utopians are always inherently reassuring. They offer hope, a nice warm feeling of certainty and are delivered with a pleasant bedside manner. Yet their answers have the infuriating habit of being within sight in the books, but just out of reach in the real world. There always seems to be an elusive mismatch between the prescriptions of the theories and the realities of the practices. It is a little like trying to find the end of a rainbow. You can see it but can never reach, touch or feel it.

A belief in grand designs is implicit in Management utopianism. Despite the evidence of history, managers in the fantasy land of theory are encouraged to think and act as though they are so wise and so intelligent they can conceive, create, design, implement, understand and manage organisational edifices of unimaginable complexity and sophistication. Politicians and their advisers also suffer from utopianism in spades. They excel at propounding grand designs and making an almighty cock-up of them.

The builders of the tower of Babel had a grand design and we know what happened to that little escapade. Then, that was a long time ago and they did not have the advantages of technology to provide instant computerised language translation! Using this kind of reasoning the explanation as to why Rome was not built in a day is because Management Utopia (circa 2015) Inc. did not do the building work!

Organisational 'folly de grandeur' is also part and parcel of Management utopianism. One of its most common manifestations is the monolithic and incredibly complex computer projects and systems, all of which are destined to end in tears. The 'experts' and gurus *know* they will work even though most previous similar attempts have ended up in ignominious and expensive failure. The questions sensible managers should ask such as 'What experience do you have of the kind of scale and size of what you propose?' and 'Who do you know who has achieved something similar?' somehow don't get asked about complex technology systems.

When the inevitable disasters happen, as they still do with depressing frequency particularly in the public sector, the standard excuse of the experts is that 'senior management did not understand or properly support us'! It is interesting how they almost always blame 'senior management' rather than 'management' and how the 'experts' never blame themselves no matter how high their fee rate. It is interesting, too, that the term 'senior management' is used so often in organisations that claim to have flat management structures. Standing tall, taking responsibility and admitting to error has little part in the lexicon of modern Management Utopianism. They blame failure on a lack of understanding by someone else. The buck never stops anywhere and is always passed on until it gets lost. Accountability is increasingly politically and managerially incorrect.

Another manifestation of the utopian folly stakes is the drug-like addiction to sweeping organisational changes. This is often master-minded (if minded is the right word, mindless would probably be more accurate) by one of the world-class management consultancy companies using their latest model or methodology.

More often than not the outcome is a game of management musical chairs that achieves little or nothing or results in chaos and decimates an organisation. One answer to the question 'how do you create a small organisation' is 'bring a team of consultants into a large one'! Any fool can change organisations, or advise how and what to change. Regrettably too many are in a position to do so and highly intelligent people are often highly foolish.

In the 1960s and 1970s, when I worked for Philips Industries, one of the operating companies within Philips UK brought in fashionable and expensive consultants to advise on reorganisation. The shambles they created was unbelievable. It really was staggering that highly intelligent managers were so out of touch with reality and so lacking in inner confidence that they put up with such nonsense and paid an outrageous sum for the privilege. I wondered then if the world of management was going mad. I sometimes wonder now if it has gone *completely* mad!

The utopian intellectual games played by the large management consultancies are mind-boggling. In the 1960's, influenced by the supposed success of Harold Sydney Geneen in ITT, they went around preaching the message of diversification, the merit of organisational bureaucracies and the need for matrix management. As a consequence large organisations added layers of management, built huge office blocks to house them and bought businesses they knew nothing about. It all ended in expensive tears and human misery.

The theoretical 'raison d'etre' underpinning this bout of utopian madness was initially provided by the Boston Consultancy Group with their four-box model. This divided companies into cash cows, rising stars, dogs and question marks. The theory was that the new conglomerates would milk the cash cows to finance the rising stars. The reality was that the so-called dogs were often the cash and profit generators. Other consultancies jumped on the Boston Grid bandwagon and dreamed up even more complicated (and more misleading) models. These were doubtless more expensive as they had more boxes!

Some of the theories are merely re-cycled old ideas and theories dressed up in shining new packages – mutton dressed up as lamb. The medium and the package, not the substance, is the message. Most, if not all, of the elements and steps in Business Process Re-Engineering (BPR) for example were described in *Introduction to Work Study* first published in 1957. The only difference is in the embellishment, hype and the extravagant claims. One of its leading proponents Michael Hammer had the gall to describe re-engineering as the most significant innovation since Adam Smith wrote *The Wealth of Nations*. Pull the other leg Mr. Hammer it has bells on it!

In fairness to Mr. Hammer his theories proved profitable - *for consultants!* William Stottard, a managing partner of Anderson Consulting, waxed lyrical saying 'God Bless Michael Hammer – because he really popularised and legitimated the concept. After his article we saw a ramping up of demand'. By 1993 Anderson Consulting was reaping $700 million of income a year from the re-engineering bandwagon.

How much the bandwagon benefited their customers, if at all, is of course, impossible to determine. If the re-engineering was done to their clients, as is too often the case, rather than with and by the clients, I would be surprised if the benefits were positive let alone significant. Too often consultants waltz in and out, pocket large fees and leave chaos behind. One former management consultant estimated that about a third to a quarter of consultancy assignments he experienced were good value, about half questionable or no value and the rest incompetent of destructive. Other studies suggest that 75% of BPR attempts fail.

Many utopian theories offer certainties when the real problems of management centre on uncertainties. They offer answers when the real problems are about coping with paradox. They proffer simplistic solutions for coping with inherent organisational complexities, which are beyond human comprehension. They profess to know what they do not know unlike Socrates who said "I know that I know nothing".

They are also highly purposeful and wedded to cause and effect as if every human action is rational and outcome orientated. The concept that success can be due to accident or serendipity is foreign to their philosophy. The theorists seemingly don't understand that all organisations are to some extent vague and confusing and necessarily so as that is part of the human condition.

It is usually considered sensible to stop digging when stuck in a deep hole. The theorists, however, dig on regardless in their never-ending quest for *the* Management Utopia, which is a moving target if ever there was one. One minute the Utopia is the Value Chain. The next minute it is the Utopia of Customer Care. Then it is the Utopia of Business Process Re-engineering (BPR), Knowledge Management or whatever is the current fashion. So it goes on in an endless series of circles.

One of the biggest dangers of all utopian theories, whether they are about management or anything else, is that they become doctrinaire belief systems with all the paraphernalia of such systems - scribes, theologians, priests, enthusiastic practitioners, true believers and converts who are more catholic than the Pope. All dogmatic systems breed fanaticism. They are inherently intolerant and totalitarian although they rarely set out to be so. As Professor John Carey pointed out 'visions of heaven soon turn into a communist hell'[i]

Two of the most able and intelligent colleagues I worked with at Digital Equipment Company Ltd., were proponents of managerial belief systems. One of my colleagues was convinced that Customer Care should be *the* universal formula for organisational success. Another believed, with equal conviction, integrity and passion that Total Quality Management should be *the* overarching managerial driving force. The latter also believed that Digital's problems (see Chapter 3) were largely due to the absence of TQM.

---

[i] John Carey *The Faber Book of Utopias* (London – Faber & Faber 1999) ISBN 0-571-19790-6

Both propounded their utopian ideals as the ultimate truth but clearly both couldn't be right. When I suggested, with tongue in cheek, to one that surely TQM should come first I was told that TQM was an outcome of Customer Care. When I suggested, also with tongue firmly in cheek, to the other that Customer Care was surely more important than TQM I was told that Customer Care stemmed from TQM. Tweedledee and Tweedledum. There was no way in logic of determining which or who was 'right' and which or who was 'wrong'. Actually there were both wrong and right!

Their replies reminded me of debates I've had in the past with committed communists in the trade union movement. The communists always came back to the hypotheses of Marx as the ultimate source of truth. Nothing could shake their circular belief systems. They also reminded me of the computer in Douglas Adam's novel *The Hitchhikers Guide to the Galaxy* which pondered the mysteries of the universe and came up with the answer 42!

In reality there is no practical difference between improving the performance of an organisation by Customer Care (which includes improving quality) or by Total Quality Management (which includes improving customer service) or by any other means provided they use common sense. Whether either is *the* answer is highly doubtful - the Holy Grail does not exist in management or anywhere else in this world. At best, either may produce some benefits provided they are properly managed and implemented. Utopias don't work and never have done.

Management is difficult enough without adding in utopian aspirations.

There is nothing wrong with belief systems per-se. We all have beliefs and belief systems. The problem in management arises when belief systems become dogmatic and prescriptive and perceived as an immutable truth or a universal panacea.

In fairness to the proponents of belief systems it should be said that some are often excellent managers because they at least believe in something *and* do something about making their utopias a reality. In the pragmatic world of management, progress in roughly the right direction — even if made in pursuit of an unattainable ideal, or an illusory utopia, or for the wrong reasons — is better than no progress at all. We need utopian ideals and utopian dreams but we also need to be acutely aware they are illusory.

No one doubts that Management thrives on the stimulus of new ideas, new approaches and new perspectives and that includes utopia and utopian ideals. At an intellectual level, management is necessarily an inquisitive and acquisitive frame of mind. Debates about new ideas and theories are often the catalyst for 'solutions' in management. If we have any sense we learn from the experiences, ideas, successes and the failures of others as well as from our own mistakes.

It is hard to avoid the conclusion that far too many utopian theories are so obsessive and so facile that they are not worth the paper they are written on. There would be wholesale nervous breakdowns if managers took seriously even a small fraction of the theories on offer. They would all be charging around in circles like headless chickens.

Perhaps the greatest problem of all with Management utopianism is that it has theorised management so much that the nature of management has changed for the worse. The whole caboodle is circular and self-sustaining. Would-be managers are indoctrinated in utopianism at the Business Schools from which more and more companies recruit their elites. The bright and the brainy in the prestigious consultancy company are recruited from the same stables. In accordance with Gresham's Law, the bad money of utopianism is driving out the good money of informed common sense. Peters and Waterman in *In Search of Excellence* claim that: 'The business schools, however, aren't running the country. Managers are.' If only that was true! Management has been hijacked by business school theories and managers are clearly no longer running the show.

There are now few organisations, of even a moderate size, which don't have on their payroll expense account theoreticians (either trained at a Business School or hankering to be sent to one at their employer's expense) whose sole role appears to be attending seminars. The numbers of these are, alas, also growing. What good they do is beyond my comprehension. Soon the question will be not how something will work in practice but if it will work in theory. The cost of the inefficiency created by utopianism is astronomical.

Management, which is primarily a practical matter, has become theorised. Instead of promoting enterprise, which is one of the prime tasks of a manager, they are promoting theories. What a glorious cock-up — such is the folly of human kind.

On a visit to a large European company a senior Director said to me "Mr Moyes, we really do believe in and are committed to Total Quality Control". With the exquisite charm, diplomacy and tact, which only a Yorkshire man like myself is capable of, I replied "I don't believe that for one moment". The Director was shocked until I explained: "Look I have heard this so often but rarely see evidence of it. If you and your board are so committed, tell me what your Directors have done to ensure the board itself uses TQC?" There was, predictably, no reply.

Later during an excellent lunch, he said "Peter, (he had forgiven my shock tactics and we were on Christian name terms by then) you know our TQC is not working as well as we hoped." I replied, "Yes, we have already agreed on that haven't we?" To the Director's eternal credit I heard a month later that, on his insistence, his Board had reluctantly discussed what they should do as a Board to improve their total quality.   'For every sinner that repenteth there is a place in Heaven'!

So far the utopians have dominated the debate about the

nature and purpose of management. Those of us who express doubts are either dismissed as Philistines, or as anti-intellectual or - the ultimate put down - as 'old fashioned' in our thinking. But we have survived the excesses of the theories of the so-called School of Scientific Management (a nonsense if ever there was one) with its mechanistic and reductionist logic and paralysis by analysis and we can temper those of Utopian Management.

The only theoretically perfect company would be a people-less-company which, of course, is an impossibility except to those utopians daft enough to believe that machine intelligence can and will displace human intelligence. Anyone who believes that — and there are some who come close to doing so — will believe anything. Perfect companies, like indispensable people, can only be found in the vanities of the mind or in the graveyard.

Truth is many sided and we all tell the side which suits us. Facts can be used to prove almost anything. In management, as in life, reality is perception and perception is the *only* reality. Managers need to rely much more on their own perceptions and much less on utopian formulas, models and theories of others, however well meaning. They need to realise that there are ultimately no answers only questions and that by 'answering' one question we simply gain the insight and wisdom to ask another. They need to realise that the solution to a problem lies not in knowing the answer, or in theorising the problem away, but in realising there is a problem and in asking the right questions to understand what the real problem is.

Utopian Illusions

The utopian quest prevalent in management theory always and necessarily ignores the reality of human nature. Management is essentially about people. People are not perfect, but instead are good and bad, often downright awkward and sometimes even wicked. They are not machines and they don't act like machines. They cannot be explained or understood by mechanistic theories or by the intellectual constructs now so prevalent. The reality is that management is a messy and imperfect business because it is about people. Management is about shades of grey and the shades are sometimes decidedly murky.

Wise managers place trust in themselves, their experience, their conviction and above in all in their people and not in the theories and models of others. They know that their success depends on a lot of hard work, informed common sense, insight, experience and wisdom and on a little bit of luck. They know that true wisdom lies in realising how little they know, not how much they know, and in a continuing desire to learn and an unquenchable thirst for knowledge. They know it is people who learn, not organisations.

Belief in ourselves and belief in people is infinitely more important, infinitely more successful, and infinitely more difficult but infinitely more rewarding than belief in utopian theories, methodologies, nostrums or panaceas. To look in a mirror and realise we have seen the enemy and it is ourselves, difficult and painful though this is, is perhaps the best way to managerial effectiveness and success.

It has the further merit that it is not such a bad philosophy for living life either. It is certainly a much better philosophy for management than the tempting but misleading allure of utopianism with its palpably false promise of a pot of gold at the end of a rainbow.

Chapter 3 - Propagation of Myths

*Life is a paradox. Every truth has its counterpart, which contradicts it; and
every philosopher supplies the logic for his own undoing*
- ELBERT HUBBARD

One of the most successful Management books ever
written is *In Search of Excellence*[i] by Peters and Waterman.
The book skilfully weaves together a compendium of
folklore and anecdotal evidence. The contents were drawn
from companies, which were adjudged to be outstandingly
successful, into a comprehensive theory and formula for
success. It provides a masterly synthesis and portrays an
almost idyllic view of management and companies at their
very best. Here, at long, long last, was *the* formula, *the*
answer and *the* explanation of managerial success based on
supposedly objective research of the crème-de-la-crème of
American companies. It was almost as if the authors had
done the impossible and found the Holy Grail of
management. But it was a paradise lost: the Garden of
Eden after Eve ate the fruit of the tree of Knowledge of
Good and Evil and tempted Adam to also succumb as the
paragraphs below explains.

Managers took to it like ducks to water because *'Excellence'*
seemed to be so sensible and accorded with their
ambitions, aspirations, hopes, pre-conceptions and values.
Academics were equally enthused as it provided a rich and
stimulating stream of ideas and anecdotal evidence and it

---

[i] *Peters and Waterman In Search of Excellence (Harper and Row: New York).
ISBN 0-06-015042.*

even had the McKinsey 7-S framework to provide the theoretical basis so beloved by academia. The book really did strike a chord and much of it still does and rightly so. By inference it bore the hallmark of McKinsey, those panjandrums and potentates of Management Consultancy. Both the authors had worked for that august institution. With such antecedents how could it be wrong? No wonder it was such a run-away success and deservedly so.

Personally I was so enthused by the book that I hankered to work for one of the world's excellent companies. Soon after I joined Digital Equipment on which this chapter is mainly based. A tiny part of me was uneasy with the perceptions Peters and Waterman had expressed about Digital. They seemed to have accurately reported what they heard or saw of the folklore, the received wisdom and the articles of faith within Digital. It made sense to them, their readers, Digital's customers and their staff.

Any doubts I had were soon swept away by the tremendous camaraderie, dedication and energy I found within Digital. It seemed to be just like Peters and Waterman said. There was a sense of purpose and shared beliefs which transcended national and other boundaries. We believed anything and everything was possible. We all really did work hard albeit sadly to little ultimate gain as events were to show.

Working for Digital was in many ways the most enjoyable, most energising, most satisfying and most productive period in my 40 year working life. The energy and folklore of Digital overcame my initial scepticism as it did for everyone else. In our exhilaration we put doubt and reason aside. Digital was a very good and very exciting company to work for. No wonder it seemed to so richly merit the accolade of excellence.

Admittedly there was a great deal of naivety and foolishness. I heard Digital staff on training courses say they 'added value' when asked what they did. One Digital senior executive told Peters and Waterman that he and a group were leaving that Thursday evening for Vail, Colorado to plan a reorganisation ('they are no fools at Digital'). The executive said 'we'll be back by Monday night, and I expect we'll announce the changes in the sales force on Tuesday. The front end of the implementation should be well in place a week or so later.'[ii]

What arrant nonsense, yet Peters and Waterman were taken in and impressed. Had they looked a little more thoroughly and seen the consequences of such foolish instant managerial decisions, as I did from time to time, they would probably have changed their minds.

It reminded me of the description, by the historian and politician Alan Clarke, of the leadership in the First World War as 'Lions led by donkeys'. Digital had lots of lions. It also had, like all organisations, a number of donkeys and some of the donkeys were alas in positions of influence and power. It was ever thus. Human folly knows no bounds.

[ii] *ibid p 129*

The growth, profitability and success of Digital had derived primarily from three remarkable innovations – the invention of the minicomputer the PDP 8, the PDP11 mini and the VAX computer – and the remarkable prescience of Kenneth Olsen its founder and Chief Executive. Olsen was an engineer's engineer. For a number of years his technical leadership and down to earth approach propelled Digital from success to success. In its heyday Digital rarely pro-actively sold its innovative products; it basically took orders.

Sadly Olsen was fallible like the rest of the human race. He ignored the threat and opportunity of UNIX and then the threat and opportunity of the Personal Computer and as a result, Digital faltered. The rest is history. Olsen described UNIX as 'snake oil' and said of PCs 'There is no reason anyone would want a computer in their home.' Sun with its UNIX based systems took market share from Digital in the same way as Digital had earlier taken business from IBM with its mini-based systems. When Digital finally took the PC market seriously it did much too little, much too late and never really understood the new market.

Until it stumbled, everything Digital touched seemed to turn to gold. To support customers, it developed support services, which were even more profitable than its products. The gross margins on activities such as VAX training were huge. Digital never seemed to put a foot wrong - success begat success, profits begat profits.

At its peak, annual compound growth reached a remarkable 20%. It had a debt free balance sheet. One commentator at the time claimed that Digital was the second fastest growing company in the history of the world (Honda, apparently was number one). Olsen was acclaimed in Business Week and appeared on the cover of Time Magazine. By any standards this was surely a success story. It would be most unfair to criticise Peters and Waterman for perceiving Digital as a company of excellence in the light of Digital's incredible growth, profitability and success and the commitment and dedication of its staff.

The reality was that Digital was nothing like the paragon of virtue described by *In Search of Excellence* and nor were the other 'excellence' companies anything like as excellent as was being suggested. The book identified eight criteria or rules for excellence and 43 companies meeting the criteria. Within a couple of years of being published, 14 of the companies were no longer meeting the criteria of excellence according to *Business Week*. The magic formula suddenly lost its magic. It was as if the Gods had tricked them and us by raising our sights and expectations and then capriciously casting them down, as Gods are wont to do. Digital was a victim of the hubris and went under. It was taken over by Compaq who in turn were taken over by Hewlett Packard.

Perfection is not within the reach of any institution created by human beings and some of the managerial nostrums propagated in *Excellence* soon looked distinctly threadbare as one of its joint authors, Tom Peters, later admitted with admirable candour and integrity.

Digital may have been the most exciting and profitable company I have worked for or with. It was also, I regret to admit, poorly managed and organised in a number of areas. There were exceptions: Field Service for instance had a refreshing no nonsense, down-to-earth approach.

The strength of Digital was centred on its founder Ken Olsen, renowned for his common sense and pragmatism, and a group of brilliant hardware and software engineers. But surrounding this core was a corporate and marketing bureaucracy, which sometimes lived in fantasyland wholly unlike the pragmatic Olsen. On one occasion an exasperated Olsen sent this memo to staff:

> *'Remember my story of how Moses came down with ten simple rules to live by and how the rabbis spent the next hundred years adding details and volumes of red tape to fill in the details that Moses could not carry down from the mountain?*
>
> *'When Christ came, he said 'I free you from all those rules; you now have freedom. In fact I have simplified Moses' rules to only two: Love God and love your neighbour.' For two thousand years, the church has been adding red tape, rules and regulations to this.*
>
> *We announced the New Management System which has freedom – no rules, no regulations, no red tape – and already you are paying the part of the rabbis and the preachers in adding new regulations, red tape and rules which never were in the New Management System.*

If we say all the new small niches have to fit into the big overhead structures, you can be sure they will never be approved and they will be stifled with overhead. Clearly, the New Management System's goal was not to have large overhead structures which make all the decisions and have absolute control over Business Units.'

Unfortunately for Digital, some corporate bureaucrats and theoreticians thought otherwise and circumvented Ken Olsen's wishes either because they did not agree or did not understand. His wishes did not fit in with their business school theories or the way they perceived Digital. It shows even the most successful companies become corporatist, theorised and mismanaged.

The management of Digital, although in my judgement sometimes naïve and impracticable, were in the main intelligent, caring and honest, much more so than in many companies I have encountered. Like Olsen himself, the managers were the prisoners of the company's run-away success. When I joined, their main preoccupation was coping with the problems of growth. Dr Johnson once remarked that 'when a man knows he is to be hanged in a fortnight, it concentrates his mind wonderfully'. The incentive to concentrate the mind hardly existed in Digital where a bright future beckoned; one where money appeared to grow on trees and to get more money it seemed only necessary to shake the trees.

Digital in its prosperous years was, like many other similar hi-tech corporations, a massive wining, dining, training and travelling club where economy and efficiency appeared unimportant. This was the side, which Peters and Waterman did not report. An essential part of Digital's folklore was 'woods meetings' (which they comment on) where an entire group would decamp to a posh hotel at considerable cost (sometimes even in another country) to commune with each other and formulate action plans which were always much more plans than action.

That, of course, is not new in large organisations. In my time at Philips Industries they used to have 'Concern Development Committees' (CDC's). For some reason, probably to do with translation from Dutch to English, Philips described itself internally as 'the Concern'. The committees were unofficially known as 'Concern Dining Clubs' — an unkind but reasonably accurate and perceptive description. At least in Philips they were limited to a small minority whereas in Digital almost everyone seemed to attend woods meetings.

Theories and theorists abounded in Digital. There were meetings, meetings and more meetings. There was travel and more travel and staff whose work-life consisted of commuting across the Atlantic. There was training in abundance. External speakers were transported across the world at huge expense to spread new ideas and messages. Star speakers demanded, and got, first class travel, even limousine transport.

New Age thinking was the vogue. I was once told I was a New Age thinker although I did not have a clue what New Age thinking was supposed to be. I certainly did not think much of it when I found out! To me it seemed like a hippie gimmick. Gurus like Donovan, MacFarlane, Porter, and Hammer were spoken of in almost hushed whispers as if they were Delphic oracles.

The theoreticians in marketing spared no expense in attempting to get reflected glory by hiring world-class speakers to entertain customers. Actually some of them were not all that entertaining. How paying large sums to speakers at customer seminars was supposed to increase sales was never satisfactorily explained. It just seemed a 'good thing' to do.

The theorists were often exasperating, obtuse and hopelessly impracticable. One group in UK marketing actually commissioned a promotional video about an achievement of one consultancy assignment we conducted for a customer without even consulting the consultants responsible for the success. People, with no practical experience whatsoever of designing and making presentations, set monolithic corporate standards for all presentation slides. My comment that they reminded me of Stalinist architecture was not well received, even though it was true!

At one time, swarms of European Staff were sent on expensive management training courses at a prestigious business school. Afterwards groups were set up to use what they had learnt and to analyse the problems of customer companies so that Digital could demonstrate it understood their business and thereby increase sales to them. Sometimes these groups bordered on black comedy. One group of whiz-kids, of whom few had any first-hand experience of management, actually discussed in all seriousness what Digital should advise the management of Glaxo to do when its patents on Zantac ran out. Fortunately that insanity was stopped before Digital made a fool of itself.

Waste was endemic. Soon after joining Digital I was nominated to speak at an international seminar for key customers and was summoned to attend a planning meeting in Geneva for the event. When I said that I had a meeting in the UK with the Board of Directors of a large and important customer I was told to cancel it! When I explained that, for me, the customer came first and there was no way I would cancel it, arrangements were made for me to dash to the airport after the meeting, leave my car in the expensive short term car park and get on the next plane no matter what.

There were no less than twenty attendee 'organisers' from all parts of Europe at the two day meeting held to review the organisation and content of the seminar. All the speakers were supposed to provide a summary of their presentation. I did not then know the ropes and I was the only one foolish enough to do so. For my pains, my presentation was promptly torn to pieces. When, in response, I unwisely told some of the critics they did not know what they were talking about there was stunned silence at such a managerially incorrect remark. It was patiently explained to me afterwards, as if I was the village idiot, that if the room cleaner had joined the meeting and made comments (however nonsensical) they still had to be treated seriously in the Digital culture.

In the event, the seminar was adjudged 'a success' by its organisers — a self-fulfilling prophecy if ever there was one. No one ever queried the costs or why it needed twenty participants to organise a seminar attended by 25 customers. Nor why 40 Digital staff needed to attend or why a small fortune was spent on external guest speakers. They had actually planned to video the whole seminar until I pointed out the cost and queried the benefits of doing so and asked who an earth would look at the videos anyway. Fortunately, my presentation received high marking from both customers and Digital attendees. Had it not done so I suspect my career in Digital would have been a short one!

Digital believed and said that the customer came first to the extent, as Peters and Waterman related, of using its customers at a technical level to evaluate and test new products. The downside was that at a human level there was frequently little or no continuity. A significant proportion of sales personnel and customer support staff were literally rotated, almost every year, from account to account very nearly as if they were playing a game of musical chairs. It seemed to me that Digital was using account rotation to foster an illusion of career progression because it was unable to offer the promotion prospects its sales and sales support staff had been led to expect.

At one point I met the Deputy Chief Executive of a large and important customer who complained bitterly and in my view rightly, that he had dealt with five different local Digital account executives in just seven years, three or four national account executives and a number of different district managers. His other computer supplier, ICL, had the same local account executive for seven years and when they first bought an ICL computer, ICL had transferred one of their key staff to the customer to manage it.

The ICL account executive understood his customer and was always coming up with suggestions and proposals to help the business. His Digital counterparts were all the time learning and then leaving for other accounts (shades of Petronius![iii]). Digital sales people *may* have gained experience from moving between different customers but that did not benefit this customer or Digital. Whereas ICL sold to its customer through experience and continuity, Digital thought it could sell by rotating its sales people and sending them on management training courses.

They also invited customer executives to attend seminars where they were treated like troglodytes and subjected to boring presentations in dark rooms. The marketing and sales plan for this account was actually based on displacing ICL. Hope springs eternal!

Some months before my visit, Digital had held a seminar for this customer to demonstrate its VAX based workstations. At the time the conventional wisdom within Digital was that VAX was good and UNIX was 'snake oil'. The customer was using UNIX based workstations because they were cheaper and faster. When a senior divisional engineering manager at the customer pointed this out to the Digital techie doing the presentation, the manager was

---

[iii] See quote chapter 7

told he did not know what he was talking about. How to win friends and influence people!

The public face of Digital was DECville (held in Cannes every two years) and DECworld (held in Boston). At these extravagant events, the company displayed its technological prowess like a male peacock displays its feathers and entertained its customers lavishly. At DECville one year, there was even a plane flying around every day pulling a DECville banner. What good that was supposed to do, I never understood. It obviously cost stacks of money but it was not really good form to ask questions about value for money.

One year, a five star luxury liner was hired for DECville staff. There were not sufficient hotel rooms in Cannes for customers and staff. I estimated it cost Digital $3,000 for each member of staff who stayed on the liner. Even when Digital fell on hard times and was cutting back on expenditure, these two events survived but staff had to put up with the 'hardship' of staying in a nearby Club Mediterranean resort. It is exceedingly doubtful whether any were ever remotely cost effective but the conventional Digital wisdom was that they were and they had figures, of sorts, to prove it. Lies, damned lies and statistics!

If all organisations could be run like Digital was, with little regard to expense, then the world of work would be much more affluent and enjoyable. It was a kind of rich Welfare State. It really was a good life. No wonder Peters and Waterman were impressed. But management and the world are not like that. Sooner or later reality intrudes. No company can forever generate large gross margins and only a few outstanding companies in exceptional market conditions do so because of their efficiency. Abnormally high margins are usually generated more by monopoly products or monopoly services or by sharp practices, such as used by banks or by branding than by excellence. When the market shifts, as it ultimately always does, competition quickly undermines monopoly prices, erodes margins and causes painful changes.

Another excellence company, the once seemingly invincible IBM, discovered this to its cost. For years IBM was the model of outstanding management for the theorists with its motto of 'THINK!' It was almost a shrine where management theorists worshipped. At its zenith it enjoyed 90% gross margins[iv] on its mainframe computer sales. Its income was greater than that of the gross national product of many small countries. In its own image, IBM's outstanding success and profitability was based on its wonderful management methods and style, its selling skills and its brilliant products. (In my view they were woefully inferior). In fact its success derived primarily from its monopoly position in the market place.

Soon after 'Excellence' was published IBM, fell off its pedestal. It saw its dominance seriously undermined (partly by the success of Digital) and posted the then biggest loss of any company in history. What price excellence then? IBM was revealed for what it was: a bloated, inefficient and self-satisfied bureaucracy stuffed

---

[iv] Only Management Consultancy companies, with gross margins of up to 80%, came close to IBM.

full of theories and theorists like its nearest competitor Digital only more so. It took leadership of the old-fashioned command and control kind (so ridiculed by modern management theorists) to rescue IBM from terminal decline.

When a dominant market position is eroded, as it was for Digital, IBM and some of the other companies identified by Peters and Waterman, there is turmoil and resentment because the hallowed values enshrined in company folklore are torn asunder. The immutable truths suddenly cease to be either immutable or true and that produces a seismic culture shock and leads to denial and all sorts of related problems including resentment and stress.

Warning signs of impending trouble are almost always obvious but everyone ignores them. It did not take a PhD to see that IBM's semi-monopoly could not continue forever. Neither does it need a genius to realise that Microsoft could not walk on water for ever. There has only been one recorded case of anyone walking on water and even that may not be accurate! Perhaps the currently all-conquering Apple should remain wary of the 'Ides of March'.

Often the writing has been on the wall for some time but, if everyone has his or her back turned to the wall, no one ever sees the writing. There are none so blind as those who do not wish to see. Some did foresee the decline of Digital although few, if any, including myself, foresaw its demise. I remember my manager, Norman Ward, who was perceptive and prescient, telling me these were the halcyon days that should be enjoyed while they lasted because, they would not last forever.

When Digital employed 120,000 people, a colleague and friend, Nicola Renshaw, did a comparison of the performances of Digital, Hewlett Packard and IBM. She compared sales per employee and capital employed per dollar of sale. Digital had significantly lower sales per employee and used proportionately more capital per dollar of sales than its two rivals. Since Digital was efficient at using working capital and used proportionately less than its rivals, the inescapable conclusion was that Digital was seriously over staffed. No amount of wishful thinking could change this. The astute Nicola estimated that to compete on level terms it needed to cut its staff by nearly half to 70,000.

Nicola's common sense calculations were hardly rocket science and could and should have been conducted by those directing the financial affairs of Digital. The figures were so alarmist that no one wanted to listen, or was prepared to listen, to such a diagnosis. It simply did not fit in with the perceived wisdom and folklore. (To be fair to the sceptics I foolishly, for emotional reasons, did not sell my shares when they were high even though I believed the figures intellectually).

Digital had never made anyone redundant. Even when Digital finally faced the need to reduce staff levels, it was seen as a small re-adjustment and the euphemism 'right sizing' was first used to describe it. After protests it was changed to 'downsizing'. Then finally, Digital called a spade a spade and used the word redundancy. They did too little too late as is invariably the case in such situations.

During a round of subsequent cuts and with knowledge of Nicola's calculations, I had the temerity to suggest to a Digital Senior Executive in the UK that the cuts needed to be much greater than announced. I was tartly told the calculations were 'theoretical'. Some theory! Four years later Digital had reduced its staff to less than 60,000 and its sales were slightly higher in money terms than when they employed 120,000. Later the miscalculations proved so serious that Digital could not survive. What a tragedy and what a salutary lesson.

In Search of Excellence and Digital's place in it, illustrates how difficult it is to understand an organisation and separate the facts from the fiction inherent in all company folklore. However objective or experienced a writer or investigator is, they rarely get a realistic multi-dimensional view of an organisation especially if they are in search of a theory. This should not be surprising nor is it new. At one time *Coming of Age in Samoa* by Margaret Mead was one of the most authoritative, impeccable and widely quoted anthropological studies but is now regarded by many as a hoax[v]. Writers in search of a theory are sometimes less than objective.

In '*Excellence*' the practice of management was supplanted by a theory that had little or no relation to reality. This is a reflection of the emphasis, in modern society, on

---

[v] Derek Freeman. *The Fateful Hoaxing of Margaret Mead: A Historical Analysis of Her Samoan Research. (Westview)* ISBN: 081335604

information, 'facts', theories and the vast accumulation of 'information' and trivia on the Internet. We appear to live in an age beset by politically correct theories. The trouble is, management is a practical matter not a theoretical or intellectual exercise.

Management is about enterprise and leadership and these don't lend themselves to simplistic and theoretical explanations or generalisations. What succeeds for one manager does not necessarily succeed for another. There is a world of difference between what a charismatic and gifted leader can persuade people to achieve and what a 'do-it-by-the-book' manager fails to persuade the same people to accomplish. The differences do not lend themselves to neat analytical boxes or theories. If management were that simple there would be no need for managerial leaders.

The cultural ambience of modern westernised societies places the emphasis more on answers than on questions. There is little or no room for the doubt, paradox and uncertainty of the real world. As one writer put it, 'A civilisation of answers cannot help but be a civilisation of swirling fads and facile emotions'[vi]. Modern management is beset in spades with them.

Management theory and hyperbole have become *the* growth industries of our time. The business schools and others churn out reams of bumf at an alarming rate. There is no escaping the reach of the theorists and theories

---

[vi] *John Ralston Saul Voltaire's Bastards (Vintage Books: 1992) ISBN 0-679-74819-9*

however outlandish or nonsensical. It seems as though many modern managerial leaders have been brainwashed to believe they cannot manage without the crutches provided by a management consultant or advisor. My belief is that good management is about throwing crutches away and developing the self-confidence of one's own staff.

The tragedy of *'Excellence'* is that it proved a rickety crutch and despite its own undoubted excellence may have unwittingly done more harm than good. The book portrayed organisational folklore and myths as reality. A diet of 'A Bias for Action', 'Stay Close to the Customer', 'Get Productivity though People', 'Have a Hands-on, Value-Driven Bias', 'Stick to the Knitting', 'Simultaneous Loose-Tight Properties' is as misleading as any other management diet. Like all diets it has a high failure rate and provides little or no permanent benefit.

Looking back, with the luxury of hindsight, it is difficult to understand why so many of us, including myself, were so foolish and so naive as to uncritically accept and believe what the book said. The confused and messy reality of organisation life is nothing like the idealised view postulated and never can be. Even the very best organisation is far from excellent.

So why did so many managers put reason and common sense aside and believe that the 'excellence' companies were any different? Why did we, in our cocoon in Digital, suspend common sense? The answer is that the cocoon was too cosy and that ultimately all human beings believe what they want to believe. We wanted to believe the fantasies of excellence even if they didn't make sense, could not make sense and were nothing like what we of anyone else had ever experienced.

Peters and Waterman were not gullible young Management Turks or inexperienced academics. They were mature and experienced professionals. They tried to be objective. They had integrity. They were innovative in the use of comparative yardsticks. A great deal of what they said was common sense. Few, if any, disagreed with their conclusions at the time. Their findings resonated with what thousands of managers, in all parts of the world, felt, thought and, above all, wished. The book was a runaway success because it met a need we all have, deep down, to *believe* in dreams and fairyland.

They and we had in our minds an idealised view of what management should be like and what they and we wanted it to be like. The wise manager knows that the search for perfection, while necessary for organisational health, is a mirage. Even the wisest manager sometimes forgets that simple truth. My message from the book is that we all need to dream but in management it is sensible to do so when we are asleep and not when we are awake.

Chapter 4 - Misleading Metaphors

Metaphor is pervasive in everyday life, not just in language but in thought and action. Our ordinary conceptual system, in terms of which we both think and act, is fundamentally metaphorical in nature.
- GEORGE LAKOFF AND MARK JOHNSON

Metaphors are the staple ingredient for management theorists and theories. The management theory industry uses them in such colossal quantities they deserve their own entry in the Guinness Book of Records.

The metaphors underpinning management theories are indiscriminately drawn from literally anything that comes to mind. They can embrace aerodynamics, behaviourism, biology, chemistry, economics, engineering, futurology, quantum physics, physics, science, social anthropology, technology to name but a few and the more absurd the better. So what new metaphors might we expect next? How about – and I've just invented these - 'the ecology of management' or the 'office-less office'? I'm not aware either has been used but no doubt some bright spark will tell me if they have or more likely will adopt one or both!

That said, metaphors *are* important. As Thomas Kuhn, the scientific historian, remarked, 'You don't see something until you have the right metaphor to let you perceive it'. The challenge then is in finding the right metaphor.

Many management theories draw heavily on technology for their metaphors. The Computer Industry is a rich source of metaphors for management theories because it has its own rich language and scientific fiction beliefs. It is also rather like the entertainment industry since it often fails to distinguish fact from fiction or fantasy from futures. Indeed, as we have already explored in Chapter 2, its utopian credentials are of the highest order.

The Computer Industry has an impeccable track record of promoting the illusion of computer led progress. It is no coincidence that the Management Myth Making Industry has grown in tandem with the computer industry. The two industries are almost soul mates. They feed off each other and vie with each other to see who can use metaphors to create the most hyperbole. This is what management theorists love to call synergy - itself a metaphor imported from the pharmaceutical industry that has become 'de-rigueur' in management-speak. The problem with synergy is that it is like the Yeti. They are both said to exist but no one has ever seen them or provided convincing proof they are real.[i]

At one time the Computer Industry used the metaphor of generations to signify phases in the evolution of the computer. These metaphors worked fairly well as short hand descriptions until hype took over and finally went berserk with the introduction of 'Fifth Generation Computers'. Otherwise sane people were led to believe that human brains would become subordinate to computers. There are still enthusiastic computer nerds who sincerely hold such beliefs. Fifth Generation Computers were poised to literally take over the world. It

---

i *I believe the credit is due to the industrialist the late Lord Hanson.*

was as if the human race was going to be managed by android computers using artificial intelligence. What an enthralling prospect. We really do live in interesting theoretical (or virtual?) times!

Scientific and technology progress is never matched by parallel progress in the human sphere. Computer-led progress always runs ahead of the human ability to understand and manage it. This is why using technology metaphors in management theory is so misleading. Because computers are fifth generation, there is no logical or other reason why people or organisations have become or will become fifth generation. There may be fifth generation computers but there are no fifth generation people. People are never going to start organising in a fifth or any other generation way. Human phenomena cannot be explained by theories conceived to explain and understand natural or scientific phenomena.

One of the most frequently used metaphors as a model for organisations in the twenty first century is the Internet network - a non-hierarchical model for modern organisations. In theory there is no leader, all communications are peer-to-peer and the Internet is self-configuring and self-repairing. This view ignores the major and growing problems of spam, trolls and viruses, the volume of abuse and fraud and the central body needed to co-ordinate the issue of e-mail addresses. No human-led organisation could possibly work like the Internet does yet it is one of the favourite metaphors for modern management theories.

Fantasy or Reality?

Let us turn to the late Professor Roger Needham, executive director of the Microsoft Research Lab in Cambridge, England. He believed that the most basic human activities of eating, procreation and sleeping are unaffected by technology and that technology has made only incremental changes to our lives rather than revolutionary ones. He was almost certainly right. He pointed out that despite all the talk of an accelerated pace of change it nevertheless took 20 years from the invention of the computer mouse to its widespread adoption[ii]. Some might unkindly add that Microsoft was partly to blame for that.

Admittedly there is evidence that scientific and man-made systems behave in similar ways and that organisations can be viewed as socio-technical systems.[iii] However, it does not follow that such similarities mean the theoretical explanations of how a clock, or a steam engine or a fifth generation computer, or a computer network, or the Internet works are necessarily good metaphors for explaining how human beings and human organisations work. There is no logical or other connection.

The application of computer metaphors at an operational level caused mayhem, as anyone familiar with the saga of computerised production control systems will be only too painfully aware. The first attempts at batch-based systems

---

ii Roger Needham – Gregynor Lectures at University of Aberystwyth, Wales Feb 2000.
http://research.microsoft.com/users/needham/text_of_three_gregynog_lectures_.htm
iii John Beishon and Geoff Peters Systems Behaviour (London: The Open University Press, Harper & Row). SBN 06-318011-1

were largely disastrous. Many were and some still are, glorified paper printing systems. The self-anointed experts (who mostly knew nothing about production but knew something about computers) next invented real time Materials Requirements Planning. Here we were told MRP was *the* answer. Then, in typical computer industry fashion and language, they revised their answer. They added bells and whistles (called an upgrade path in computer-land speak), labelled it MRP II and changed the acronym to Management Resource Planning.

These systems were claimed to pull everything together and ensure everything worked to the same grandiose game plan. Far from pulling things together the vast majority of the many I saw, pushed them apart. They often created complexity, produced a forest of paperwork and caused almighty confusion far worse than Petronius (see chapter 7) could have imagined even in his worst nightmare.

For years MRP held sway in Western companies, despite its evident inferiority to the common sense JIT (Just-in-Time) systems used by the Japanese. MRP provided a good living for an army of experts, gurus and theoreticians. As a result of my experience with these systems I, like Petronius, learned later in life that experts (and particularly computer experts) should always be on tap and never on top. It is a lesson I commend to all managers and would-be managerial leaders.

The other lessons we need to learn are to use metaphors with caution and with care and not indiscriminately.

Scientific analogies especially do not directly translate into social and managerial theories. People are not computers or machines and, thank goodness, never will be. No one can understand management purely by metaphors. At best the *right* metaphors may help. At worst the *wrong* metaphors lead to theories bearing little or no relationship to the effective practice of management in the real world.

Chapter 5 - Training Mumbo-Jumbo

However much thou art read in theory, if thou has no practice thou art ignorant
— SA'DI (1184-1291), PERSIAN POET

Astronomical sums are spent on the mumbo-jumbo of management training. The training arm of the Management Myth Making industry is huge and is reported to be worth as much as $60 billion a year in the US alone.[i] Lord Lever, who founded Lever Brothers (now Unilever), once said that half the money spent on advertising was wasted but unfortunately, he did not know which half.

If my experience of management training is any guide, the proportion of the money wasted on training outdoes advertising by a huge percentage margin.

Of the innumerable training courses, seminars and workshops I have attended in my career, only a handful were any good. This experience is not exceptional or unusual. In the late 1980s Xerox put approximately 70,000 staff through six-day 'quality' training courses.

Assessment interviews after the training revealed how ineffective the training had been with only 13 per cent

---

[i] *Estimates of this kind need to be treated with a great deal of scepticism. This figure was quoted by Jeffrey Pfeffer and Robert I Sutton in The Knowing-Doing Gap – How Smart Companies Turn Knowledge into Action (Boston: Harvard Bus School Press 2000) ISBN 1-57851-124-124-0 p1.*

reporting that they used 'cost of quality' in their decision making[ii].

If anything has a novelty value and attracts the punters then, in the fantasy world of the Management Myth Making Industry, it is management training. This includes bonding, using clowns, whispering to horses, orienteering, outbound courses, motivating through music and so on. What will they dream up next?

During one period of good harvests in Philips Industries, management training was dished out like army rations. A group of behavioural psychologists secured the ear of senior management and were given free-reign to use Philips as a test bed for their theories.

Senior managers were sent on their asinine five-day 'training' courses. When they arrived they were put into groups and given a task to do without any organisation, structure or leadership. Each group had a behavioural psychologist as a passive facilitator who was strictly neutral on virtually everything that was said or done. Their object in life seemed to be to keep their cool whatever happened. If the hotel burnt down they would have doubtless said it was unfortunate and behaved with studied indifference.

Mayhem ensued as individual participants (who were all in positions of responsibility) indulged in power struggles to impose their leadership on their groups. Some sulked,

---

[ii] *ibid p 37*

some were visibly distressed. Others walked out and returned hours or even days later but no one seemed to mind. Many lost their tempers. Most got emotional. I am not sure if any were permanently harmed by the experience but it would not surprise me if some were. Many reading this will have had similar experiences.

It was never clear what the purpose of the 'training' was. I was a Senior Manager in Philips at the time and could not discern any benefit whatsoever but I did see some of the problems caused for some of my managers. Goodness knows what we were supposed to learn or how it would improve our managerial performance.

The tightly knit group, who ran the courses, were like extremist-sect fanatics and had a circular and closed belief system. When I said to one (in language which would now be considered highly politically incorrect) 'you are a thorough going bitch,' I was put comprehensively in my place by the laconic reply 'that's an interesting observation'. Touché! It was only possible to communicate with the trainers on *their* terms in accordance with *their* belief system. None of them, of course, had any first-hand experience of management but all of them were thoroughly indoctrinated in the correct behavioural approach.

One would like to think that this kind of indoctrination training is rare but unfortunately it isn't. For some years the education standards in the UK fell alarmingly because theorists got the upper hand and indoctrinated the educational system with all kinds of hocus-pocus. What mattered was not the quality of teaching but whether it was deemed to be politically correct or not. The school inspection system was largely ineffective. Bad teachers could only be removed by bribing them with early retirements on grounds of supposed ill health or other specious reasons. It was only when a determined government imposed independent assessments - in face of bitter opposition from a vocal minority of doctrinaire teachers — that standards started to improve. Some schools still suffer from the decline in standards and if my grandson is a guide, children don't seem to be traditionally taught tables and arithmetic any more.

In many large organisations, management training is the subject of similar kinds of doctrinaire pressures. Trainers with belief systems are far too common and they frequently put a particular point of view or advance their personal and utopian belief systems. Too often there is no one to curb their excesses. This was certainly the case in Digital where so-called management training was politically correct as it was in almost all the large multi-nationals I have worked with as a consultant.

The unspoken tenet of the training arm of the Management Myth Making Industry is that theorists and trainers with no practical experience of management can teach management from the book. Some even claim they can train leaders but as Warren Bennis once pointed out, 'More leaders have been made by accident, circumstance, sheer grit or will than have been made by all the leadership courses put together.' Nelson Mandela or Winston Churchill never attended training courses on management or leadership.

The ability to lead is innate. It is an aptitude some have and others don't. The idea that people learn to manage or lead is fallacious. We can, of course, all improve our skills as managerial leaders through learning, doing and practical teaching. Those without an innate aptitude for managerial leadership however, cannot lead no matter how many management-training courses they attend although some try hard. As Peter Drucker commented leadership 'cannot be taught or learned'.[iii] Explanations about how leaders lead may add to the sum of human knowledge but they don't in themselves make natural leaders.

In my youth I learned to play the cornet but despite my love of music and despite practice and teaching I did not have the aptitude to become a good cornet player. I had poor co-ordination and could not reach the top notes of a soloist. In fact I rose to the giddy heights of third cornet (playing the 'Tut Tut' bits!) in the Mirfield Baptist Military Band.

I had excellent tuition from a first-class cornet player and gifted teacher Jack Clark who tried in vain to pass on his experience and skills to me. Those who purport to provide management training mostly don't have any experience or

---

[iii] *Peter Drucker The Practice of Management (London: Mercury Books 1961) p137*

skills in management remotely comparable to Jack's in music. Too often management training is provided by those who don't 'do', never have done and never could do.

It is relatively easy to find out if a person has an aptitude for something like music or mathematics. They either have or they haven't. If they have, then their performance can be enhanced and improved by coaching, practice and teaching. But how do you measure an aptitude for management and leadership and develop and practice the aptitude? Leadership is the most ambivalent and elusive of human qualities.

The academic and training theorists ignore this reality in one of three ways. One of the ways is to disdainfully dismiss the need for managerial leadership as old-fashioned command and control management (a real 'no-no' in managerially correct circles). That view does not accord with either common sense or experience and I know of no evidence to support it.

The second way is to identify so-called "seismic shifts" created by technology and define, ex- cathedra, the 'core competencies' managers need to cope with them. These, to put it mildly, are a variable feast and are not based on any verifiable, empirical evidence but they do provide a box of goodies for new management trainers. One book identifies no less than nine core competencies it claims are needed for leadership training programmes in the 'Post-Industrial Era' whatever that is supposed to be. The nine are: Balancing stakeholder interests; Managing Conflict;

Coaching; Environmental scanning; Pattern recognition; Managing Complexity; Building shared visions; Story telling; and Systems thinking. I am afraid they do not make much sense to me. People adapt and evolve naturally to changing circumstances. They don't do so because of an unproven and un-provable hypothesis or theory. The real world is not like that.

The third way, a variant on the second, is to analyse the characteristics of industrial and other leaders who are widely acknowledged for their successes and use them as role models as the basis for training leaders in mechanistic terms.

The results are incorporated into one of the innumerable leadership cookbooks. These are the staple diet of management trainers. Virtually all suggest anyone can become a successful manager by doing what their book claims the great and good do. Although attractive intellectually at a superficial level, the flaws in this approach are so numerous as to be singularly unconvincing.

The analysis and selection of the great and the good leaders is always subjective and even worse a question of fashion. I have seen leaders who were once widely acclaimed as *the* role model for aspiring managers in a comparatively short period of time then become widely criticised and dismissed as yesterday's men or women.

Common sense suggests it is clearly preferable to deify the great and the good of management when they are safely dead than when they are alive and never to deify martyrs. The training industry needs and insists on live exemplars for its theories and nostrums and if necessary has no compunction about creating them in the same way as Hollywood creates film stars.

Management heroes have to have a fairy tale aura of invincibility. Human nature being what it is, there is always a degree of awe and sycophancy, which attributes any and every success to the heroes but never failures. Thus the British Sunday Times portrayed Bill Gates of Microsoft as a 'net prophet' even though he was late jumping onto the Internet bandwagon. It said 'He is fabulously rich, phenomenally smart and has a vision that will revolutionise our lives'. But then Messrs Marx, Lenin and Stalin also had a vision to revolutionise our lives and look how their visions turned out!

At the beginning of his career Mr Arnold Weinstock was widely admired for his achievements in creating GEC. At the end of his career Lord Weinstock was no longer thought of as a role model and was criticised (in my view unfairly) for his caution and financial prudence. That was until the critics saw what the dunderheads who took over from him did to ruin Marconi. They inherited a cash rich company from Weinstock and by a remarkable feat of incompetence, turned it into a debt ridden company owing $4.5bn (£3bn) and reduced the value of shares from over £10 ($15) each to virtually zero.

Harold Sydney Geneen was at one time lauded as *the* industrial leader and management exemplar par excellence. His company, ITT, was described as 'The Sovereign State'[iv] and not without good reason. Yet no one in his or her right mind would nowadays suggest him as a management role model.

The role model approach is fatally flawed. The 'ape the great leader' premise is akin to claiming that it is possible, by careful study, to learn how to compose like Beethoven, paint like Renoir, write like Shakespeare, invent like Edison, lead as well as President Reagan, or make money like Gates, or become a towering intellect like Newton. All this achieved by simply studying what they did and how they did it. Yet the essence of these, or any other gifted humans, is that they were, or are, exceptional and gifted. That is why they are what they are, or were, and why the rest of us are what we are.

Many leader-heroes are often mavericks. Nelson at the Battle of Copenhagen put a telescope to his blind eye when there was a signal telling him to break off battle, something he had no intention of doing. There is no way anyone can teach someone to be a Nelson or identify his core competencies. The notion is preposterous.

Obviously we can clearly all learn something from the experiences, methods and mistakes of gifted leaders but we can never possess their gifts. Bismarck believed "Only

---

[iv] Anthony Sampson *The Sovereign State – The Secret History of ITT (Coronet Books/Hodder Fawcett Ltd: London 1974)* ISBN 0 340 18284 9

a fool learns from their own mistakes. The wise man learns from the mistakes of others." The best way of learning is to do and teach what you do. I studied economics for four years but I only started to really understand it when I had to teach it to a group of accountants who had to achieve "A" level standard in less than 8 months starting from scratch. (For the record most of them succeeded!).

Sir John Harvey-Jones wrote 'my own experience of trying to teach and train managers is that it is an extremely difficult experience to teach grown-up people anything. It is, however, relatively easy to create conditions within which people will teach themselves'[v] and why teaching is only effective when student-centred rather than lecture based.

The best advice to any manager or aspirant managerial leader is to be yourself, play to your strengths and not your weaknesses. Above all, don't fall into the trap of supposing management training will solve your problems. We all learn from others but there is no way we learn by uncritically aping others or by trying to be what they are and what we are not.

As John Harvey-Jones put it: 'Management and industrial leadership is an art, not a science. Each of us approaches the problem from a different background and each of us is dealing with a different situation, a different culture and from a different starting point. There are, of course, common points and common factors which apply to us all,

---

[v] *John Harvey-Jones ibid 26*

but prescribed systems of management are seldom transferable'[vi]. Yet this is precisely what many leadership and training gurus are trying to do.

Most managers instinctively believe management training is a 'good thing', especially if they can leave the nitty-gritty to someone else. Instead of facing the underlying dilemmas, which cause so much training to be a waste of money, they are happy to go along with training when times are good (and training is, in truth, often handed out as a perk) and make savings on training when times are bad. Anyone who *really* believed in the effectiveness of training would, of course, do the reverse. In practice, few do.

The dilemmas and the problems associated with management training arise partly because of the divide between theory and practice. There is a world of difference between learning or reading about how to do something and actually doing it. The first needs the ability to learn, read and understand. The second needs these abilities plus aptitude, experience and determination.

It is, for example, relatively easy to understand project management techniques and not too difficult to learn how to use project management software. Yet understanding or learning is a far cry from being a good project manager. No one can teach aptitude and the best people to impart experience are gifted project managers (who are rare and

---

[vi] *John Harvey-Jones ibid p 27*

worth their weight in gold) not professional trainers with little or no actual experience.

The fault line in most management training is that, in line with politically correct cultural norms, it concentrates on teaching the theories in an academic or pseudo-academic way and neglects teaching *how* to implement them. If trainers taught practical implementation as well as theory, the flaws in the theories would quickly become apparent. The problem is that most management trainers have no practical experience. They do not seem to understand that intellectual understanding is a far cry from practical application.

Training a significant proportion of staff in hard subjects such as *how* to implement say 'six sigma' quality methods, as an integral part of the introduction of better quality and service, can produce amazing results provided the training also motivates. Training in the theory of 'six sigma' at best promotes some understanding. Training in tangible, factual based topics such as understanding accounts clearly has utility and value for aspirant managers and others.

Theoretical management training is abstract and its value cannot be directly assessed. However, if the contention in this book is correct, that many modern theories are gibberish or unproven and un-provable, then there is clearly little benefit in promoting the training of theoretical nonsense.

This is not to suggest there is no value in the ability to think, conceptualise and create, which learning theories stimulate. My weakest subject at university was Philosophy but it has had more influence on my career and management style than anything else - it taught me how to think in conceptual terms. A bias towards theory (however interesting or stimulating) is not the way to get something done.

Trainers think they know (or, even worse, *know* they know) a) what to train and b) how to train. The majority have no experience of actually leading and managing. They are predominantly theorists not doers and their biases are almost always towards the theoretical rather than the practical. Why have a simple practical answer when there is a complicated theoretical one available?

Successful managers know they don't know and this is one reason why they are successful. They mostly believe managerial leadership is an inherited aptitude and/or temperament, not an acquired skill. There is not a consensus on what makes a good leader but most would probably broadly agree that successful leaders have core 'doing' skills such as a persuasive personally, a think to do intellect, high levels of nervous and physical energy, optimism, confidence, an ability to see the wood for the trees, decisiveness and above all robust health. The list is not exhaustive and different managers will include different attributes. The point is that few or any of them are skills that can be taught or learned.

Like belief systems, training functions are self-justifying. The usual method of justification is to ask (i.e. insist) that delegates on their courses fill in standard assessment forms known as 'happy sheets' at the end of each course. This, of course, ensures their courses are popular since unless a course is really awful, attendees are generally kind in their assessments. Few people who spent a couple of days to a week on a training course in a comfortable hotel say it was a waste of time. There is rarely any attempt to measure whether the training was practical, relevant or useful to the organisation.

By using pre and post competency assessments, Tony Corbin, a colleague of mine in Digital, was able to demonstrate to Cabinet Office mandarins that the 1,000 plus civil servants who went through Email/Office training came out being able to do more than when they went in.

The importance of good audience assessment is key to anyone engaged in training or giving presentations. On the day before I left Digital I gave two customer presentations and was determined to go out on a high. When I saw the assessment of the morning session I was depressed to have got such a low assessment when I had been used to getting high ones. In the afternoon I really pulled the stops out and used all the rhetorical and presentations skills I knew. I really did try to walk on water and literally had the audience eating out of my hand.

The afternoon assessments seemed hardly better than the morning ones until I realised that an administrator had introduce new assessments forms with the high assessments on the left instead of on the right. It just goes to show how important the quest for ratings is. But we should all be clear that an ability to secure a high audience rating might only mean the speaker is a good entertainer and not necessarily a good trainer. All that glitters is not gold although I am glad I glittered on that occasion!

I learned how little audience ratings mean when giving seminars on 'Learning from the Japanese' in the 1980's. Feedback was excellent but in following up the seminars (itself a rarity in training) I found that less than 1% of the audiences did anything at all as a result of attending a seminar. At a guess only 0.1% made measurable achievements. This at a time when the performances of swathes of British Industry were pathetic when compared to their Japanese competitors.

Many assessment forms are of no practical value. The ones used in Digital for management consultancy training had been devised for assessing the training of technicians and engineers and were almost totally irrelevant. Despite this the training bureaucrats insisted we fill them in. They appraised their trainers mostly on the results of the assessments and whether the trainers had filled in all the right forms and had a proper course plan etc.

Following the procedures was almost as important, or even more essential, than the quality of the training as one of my colleagues and friends Ioan Tenner (a gifted trainer) found to his cost. He fell foul of the ubiquitous system and his unimaginative management and was penalised for doing so. They had the quaint notion that provided there was adequate course material any management trainer can teach almost anything.

Three bright colleagues and friends – John Geesink, Bonnie Sontag and Charles Revkin developed an innovative management consultancy technique called TOP Mapping.™ Predictably, the Educational and Training Services establishment in Digital Europe wanted to take over the training of this powerful and successful technique in spite of the fact that it had no experience of management consultancy. To them it was simply training and that was the end of the matter.

Had Educational Services succeed in delivering the training, TOP Mapping would certainly have been much less successful and would have probably failed. It would have been a nine-day training wonder and then would have been replaced by the next training gimmick. In the event, after a fierce internal political struggle, the inventors secured agreement that the training would be provided by mature, experienced, senior consultants rather than by young, inexperienced trainers. The training organisation would instead do the logistics. John and his colleagues insisted that only the best consultants should do the training. Furthermore one of the two consultant trainers who ran the training was often a consultant who had attended an earlier training course who had used the technique.

This approach had two results. First, the technique developed organically because of the continual input of new experiences and new ideas from newly trained users. The learning and development process was really incredible and although the original principles remained the same, the innovations and improvements were extensive.

Secondly, because the most experienced consultants were used, participants really learnt new skills and they knew the techniques were grounded in reality. Instead of learning by the book, they learned from the experience (and mistakes) of others, which is always a good thing to do. The whole approach was dynamic, energising and engaging.

When the technique was adopted by Digital in the USA, regrettably the training establishment there won the political battle and took it over. As a result the training was frozen in a time warp and did not develop or improve. It was a pale imitation of the continuous development and learning process enjoyed in Digital, Europe.

At one time my colleague Noreen Kennedy and myself actually re-trained a group of American consultants in TOP Mapping™ who had been through the American training experience. They were astonished at the way the technique had matured, how much better practical training by a practical and experienced consultants was over that provided by their professional trainers. Some other consultants who attended the standard and mechanist by-the-book training at about the same time were indignant when they heard from their colleagues about the European provided training.

There are, of course, many gifted professional trainers who teach from within rather than from a training manual or text. But if gifted trainers train topics or skills which are not relevant to the reality of Management their training will be mainly wasted. This is the nub of the problem: deciding which training is relevant to managers and would-be managerial leaders. That should be a decision for management but nowadays it is unfortunately usually a decision made by training experts. We have the absurd situation where trainers, with theoretical knowledge of management but with little or no practical experience of the sharp end, decide what should be taught to and about the sharp end.

The skills and techniques management trainers think managers ought to learn are frequently the ones not used by successful leaders. Trainers train the skills and techniques they believe managers *should* need, or ones in their comfort zones, or the ones they think will sell.

There is an inverted 80:20 rule at work in training. Trainers believe that theories and techniques comprise about 80% of successful managerial leadership so that is what they train. The contention in this book is that 80% is about the softer and largely ignored aspects of managerial leadership namely, informed common sense, intuition, good judgement, people skills, practical experience and wisdom. Sadly these are not what the text books describe or explain. How, for goodness sake, do you train someone to be wise? They either are or they are not.

One of the perennial favourites of trainers is Presentation Skills. Despite this, possibly fifty per cent of outstanding managerial leaders have poor presentational skills. There is no evidence that skill in making presentations is an essential for successful managerial leadership. I have met and worked with many excellent managers who were not endowed with exceptionally good presentational skills.

Two of the most successful British Industrial Leaders, "Tiny" Rowlands of Lonrho and Lord Weinstock of GEC, were notoriously shy and used others to present their companies. Rowlands for some years used Edward du Cann, a Member of Parliament, as his spokesman and Weinstock used to rely on his Chairman. Sir John Harvey-Jones of ICI, by contrast, had excellent presentational skills. Such is the growth and dominance of theory and training that according to Professor H Edward Wrapp of the University of Chicago, 'In some organisations, they [i.e. managers] can succeed if they are simply good at making presentations to the board of directors or writing strategic plans. The tragedy is that these talents mask real deficiencies in overall managerial capabilities. These talented performers run for cover when grubby operating decisions must be made. They often fail miserably when they are charged with earning a profit, getting things done and moving an organisation forward'[vii].

One of the many absurdities in management training are courses on bonding. Bonding is instinctive. From time immemorial, human beings have bonded together within families and tribes. We are by nature tribal. We are social creatures and bond together not merely for survival but because of what and who we are. No one with any sense would try to teach Grandma how to suck eggs. Yet trainers without sense, believe there is a need for training in how to bond. That would only makes sense if the majority of the human race was seriously dysfunctional.

Another perennial management training favourite is creativity. These courses explain the differences between convergent thinking (analytical thinking) and divergent thinking (creative thinking) and how to think creatively. They usually include a little theory on how the mind works and teach formal creativity techniques such as attribute listing, brainstorming, forced relationships, morphological analysis and synergy listing.[viii]

Creativity training is sold by extolling the virtues of a creative organisation and by implying that by sending

---

[vii] *Quoted by Peters and Waterman ibid p 36.*

[viii] *See J G Rawlinson Introduction to creative thinking and brainstorming (British Institution of Management Foundation: London 1971) ISBN 0 85946 1149 for an excellent introduction. For those with a deeper interest in creativity Arthur Koestler The act of creation (Pan Books Ltd: London 1966) is hard to beat.*

enough staff on the courses, an organisation will release enormous creative energies, literally overnight.

The reality is, of course, that people in an organisation only start to use their creative abilities if they have a creative leadership and management culture where they work, which encourages, rather than inhibits, creativity. Creativity starts with belief at the top, not by sending those at the bottom on training courses. This is not to deny the value or attractions of many interesting and useful courses on creativity, but it is to point out that training is not the way to generate a creative organisation (or individuals).

Training does, of course, cover a multitude of sins. Sometimes training is an excuse for a jamboree where the real purpose is to develop camaraderie, exchange experience and ideas and reward good performance without stimulating the taxman to ask awkward questions about benefits in kind.

Like most other managers I have taken part in and enjoyed such events as both a participant and speaker. At Digital I once, to my astonishment, "won" an award for excellence. I was rewarded by a business-class flight for my wife and myself for a four day stay in a luxury hotel in Acapulco, Mexico along with hundreds of other winners from all parts of the world. We really did live it up and to keep it legal, from a tax point of view, there were a few management lectures on the programme. However, these were not treated seriously and in reality attendance at them was voluntary. I cannot with hand on heart say the event had anything to do with management training or learning, but we both greatly enjoyed it. Who wouldn't?

On another occasion I was one of two guru guest speakers at a materials management conference of a well-known international company. The role of the guest speakers was to provoke, stimulate and entertain. The 74 delegates spent two days in a pleasant ambiance at an Oxford College hearing from the speakers on why they should learn from the Japanese. They then had to devise their own plans for doing so.

One report afterwards in the trade press was headed 'Company faces Japanese challenge.' In fact, as far as I am aware, they did nothing of the sort. They came, they heard, they discussed and then they went away happy and self-righteous. The conference possibly had a value in stimulating the delegates and in providing an opportunity for the delegates from 24 operating divisions to meet and swap experiences. It certainly did not result in them improving their competitive performance one jot.

Many seminars often turn out in similar vein and are an excuse for a pleasant day or a couple of days out listening to entertaining speakers and dining and wining well. Some of those who attend do so as a perk. Others are pseudo-academics whose objective in life seems to be to attend as many seminars as possible and to do as little as possible about them afterwards. The higher the price the more attractive the professional seminar attendees find the seminars.

The truth is there is no substitute for action and on the job learning. Too many training courses are theoretical constructs and divorced from the real world of action. Learn-do-learn-do is hard to equal let alone beat. That we have so little action based training and so much theoretical training is a consequence of the way management has been sucked towards the vortex of a black hole by theory.

When I was a consultant specialising in Japanese Methods of Management, I ran a two-day training workshop for a group marketing telephones. They were young, energetic and as bright as buttons but when I asked questions I found that none of them had ever actually sold a telephone in their lives. So, as part of the workshop, I divided them into small groups, provided each group with simple tools and two of their top selling phones. I got each group to list and count all the components and using the cost information I provided, they had to estimate the manufacturing cost of each telephone.

To start with some groups did not even manage to correctly count the number of components. When that was put right the groups came up with cost calculations and found that while the phones had the same cost, they were paying a pound more for one than the other. This meant that the selling price of one product was £34.95 and of the other £39.95 yet they were functionally the same. Hardly rocket science. Afterwards they went back to the expensive manufacturer and secured a reduction of a pound and saved a substantial sum for their company.

This is the kind of common sense hands-on 'learning to do' training that *is* worthwhile. It was based on a method of electronic function analysis and design devised by a former colleague, Tony Headley, who was one of the brightest engineer-managers I have had the privilege of working with.

Management training will continue to be a huge wasteful black hole unless managers ensure that it has a hands-on-approach directly related to real-world organisational needs. They could do no better than follow the hands on approach of Jack Welch at GE who took part in or lead 250 training session for 15,000 managers. Management training will then become an asset rather than a cost.

Chapter 6: Going Backwards

Everything seems amazing when you see the view through Rose coloured glasses – KELLY ROWLAND

The conventional wisdom is that management is now so much better than the management of our forefathers. This is attributed to the vast and growing number of articles, books and seminars on management allied to our advanced technologies. This rose-tinted view ignores the reality that human nature, and therefore management, changes and evolves slowly if at all.

It is true however that ours is a golden age of unparalleled and accelerated scientific advancement and innovation in virtually every field of science. We have reached a critical mass built upon the accumulation of knowledge over the centuries. Science fiction has in some cases become scientific fact. It is almost as if the impossible has happened. Science suddenly gelled together in a virtuous circle, has created previously undreamed of possibilities and opportunities.

Managerially, the upside of these developments is that we have been able to create systems, particularly those based on information technology, which would have been impossible a few decades ago. The options technology offers managerial leaders in a whole host of areas are now almost unlimited and well beyond the comprehension of previous generations of managers.

The downside is the growth of bureaucracy that both information and communication technology have made possible. As a consequence we have become submerged in paper and the tyranny of e-mails 24-7 (detailed in chapter 7) that destroy the boundaries between work life and home life. The health service, for example, has become a giant bureaucratic paperwork generator. In the UK, teachers are overwhelmed by paperwork and student 'face-to-face time' has reduced significantly. Put another way, productivity has suffered with outputs and service levels both falling. It is the same practically everywhere. The motif of the world of management and organisation is now information, paper and theory.

Some nevertheless succumb to the belief that technological and scientific advances have resulted in comparable advances in management. Nothing could be further from the truth. Seeing the world through rose-coloured spectacles is not very sensible. Managerial effectiveness may actually have declined steeply as theory and paperwork have taken over.

Despite the claimed advances, human beings are sadly no less prejudiced or bigoted. Our actions, individually and collectively, are still sometimes despicable. Human nature is very much as it always was and so consequently is managerial leadership. The scope for fraud in manipulating financial markets has increased exponentially and cynicism and dishonesty in management has certainly grown apace.

In terms of managerial leadership skills there is also little, that modern managers could teach those who, for example, managed and organised the design and building of the Aztec Temples.

On the other hand we could possibly learn a thing or two from the Aztecs about the design of buildings to withstand earthquakes. One of the few monuments of human endeavour and managerial organisation visible from space is the Great Wall of China - the largest known building programme ever undertaken. That did not need a theory; just determination, superb logistical organisation, leadership plus a lot of slaves or serfs with a plethora of shovels. Incidentally, it is sobering to learn that the Chinese invented and practiced mass-production techniques centuries before Henry Ford did.

The Arsenal of Venice sustained the Venetian Empire for 600 years. No modern organisation, other than the Catholic Church, can boast a life of 600 years. The Japanese company Mitsui probably comes second with a business lineage stretching back 300 years. In contrast, according to Professor Richard Foster from Yale University, the average lifespan of a company listed in the S&P 500 index of leading US companies has decreased by more than 50 years in the last century, from 67 years in the 1920s to just 15 years today. Of the nine companies or subsidiaries I have worked for in my working life, only one now exists possibly because it became a subsidiary of a South Korean company.

At its peak the Arsenal of Venice employed 20,000 people who turned out a fully equipped trading-cum-fighting ship every half day. They probably used just-in-time (JIT) methods, which we usually suppose were invented in the 1960s by the Japanese. Actually they only re-invented them though it took their Western competitors at least ten years to start to get the JIT message.

On 28th July 1850 Joseph Paxton, who began his career as a humble gardener, was awarded the contract to build an innovative iron and glass building in Hyde Park, London for the Great Exhibition of 1851. Workmen began to move onto the site two days later on 30th July 1850. The structure of Crystal Palace (six times the size of St Paul's Cathedral which incidentally took 35 years to build) was completed in January 1851 and exhibits started to be accepted on 12th February 1851 . Management and organisation was superb. The cast iron frames were fixed in place within 18 hours of leaving Birmingham by train (Just-in-Time again!). The company producing the sheet glass manufactured more in 5 months than the entire industry normally made in a year.

All this was achieved without telephones (not even ubiquitous mobiles!), electricity, fax, health and safety regulation, machines, photocopiers, personal organisers, personal computers, pocket calculators, political correctness, planning regulations, management consultants, management books, management theorists and theories, formal management techniques or Harvard Business School case studies that are all 'de rigueur' nowadays.

Most organisations would find it impossible today to design and erect an 800,000 square feet exhibition centre in such a time scale, even with the benefit of modern technology and all the paraphernalia of modern management. The exhibition was a run-away success. During the 140 days it was open it attracted 6.5 million visitors (more than the Millennium Dome, Greenwich, London attracted in 365 days from a much larger population!). It seems also to have influenced visitor numbers to the British Museum, since they soared to 2,527,216 in 1851 and it was not until 1923 that the Museum next attracted even a million visitors a year. Anyone who studied the management of the design and building of Crystal Palace would learn more from so doing than from a hundred contemporary books on management theory.

Afterwards the building was dismantled and re-erected at Sydenham on the outskirts of London and survived until 1936 when it was unfortunately destroyed by fire. The exhibition was financed by private subscriptions and took £356,000 in entry fees (the equivalent of £19 million, or $28.5m, in today's money). The surplus of £187,000 ($280,500) was used by its Commissioners to buy 87 acres of land in South Kensington: the site for London's great museums, Imperial College, the Royal College of Art, the Royal College of Music and other institutions.

The modern equivalent of Crystal Palace, the Millennium Dome, is about the same area as Crystal Palace and was a fiasco from beginning to end. This started with the lunatic decision to plan and finance it on the basis of 12 million paying visitors. It really is amazing how the great and good in society, who are often highly intelligent, can make such stupid decisions and act so foolishly. Even Tony Blair admitted, "If I had my time again, I would have listened to those who said governments shouldn't try to run big visitor attractions." He can say that again!

Financial controls were virtually non-existent. The clueless management thought their total assets were worth £240m ($360m) on 31st July 2000 whereas their real worth was a tenth of this at £24.6m ($37m). The estimates of income were way out and the maintenance department spent £1m ($1.5m) per month more than the amount budgeted. The management of the Dome, led by a former highflying civil servant, could not even organise the opening ceremony. Guests were kept waiting for hours to pass security checks. Poor Joseph Paxton must have turned in his grave at such appalling and disgraceful mismanagement.

After the dome fiasco, the British Olympic Games in 2012 were widely acclaimed by the media and politicians as a triumphant success. In managerial terms it was a disastrous example of public sector and political incompetence on a mega scale conveniently masked by the euphoria that the games themselves generated. The original budget was £2.4bn but incredibly it cost over £11bn yet some parts of the media hailed it as £528m under budget. There used to be lies, damned lies, and statistics. There are now fairy tales and hype by both politicians and the media!

Politicians and civil servants the world over are, of course, notorious for their ability to mismanage projects like the Dome as they always have done. They turn them into a bureaucratic nightmare and a costly shambles then deny any knowledge or responsibility afterwards and pass the buck elsewhere.

This phenomenon of governmental crass mismanagement is not new or unique to Britain. It is, sadly, a worldwide phenomenon although I sometimes fear, in moments of frustration, that the UK may have the dubious distinction of being the world leader in this area. In 1975 Senator William Proxmire instituted a monthly 'Golden Fleece Award' for the most self-evidently wasteful piece of American government funded spending.

One of the awards went, unbelievably, to a taxpayer funded research project costing $25,000 to study why people cheat and act rudely on Virginia tennis courts. The emphasis on management by administration in the public sector instead of management by leadership is clearly a contributory factor to the decline of managerial leadership.

Large bureaucracies in the private sector are often no better than public bureaucracies. Because they operate with much less public scrutiny, they are able to bury some of their follies and stupidities rather better.

British Airways squandered millions re-launching their image by painting the tailfins of their aircraft with a widely disliked logo. Large bureaucracies of all kinds, private or public sector, are almost always unmitigated bad news for consumers and society but of course good news for the bloated, bureaucratic elites within them.

Until the Enron fraud, the Marconi and World.com fiascos, the private sector mismanagement horror story of all time was the bizarre management inspired $25bn leverage buyout of Nabisco in 1988[i]. That really did defy belief and reason in a mega way.

Nero apparently fiddled while Rome burnt. The management of Nabisco went further than Nero and did the equivalent of pouring fuel on the flames. Banking and consultancy fees for the buyout came to a staggering $1bn - the gravy train of all gravy trains. When the deal was finally consummated it needed a meeting of no less than 200 lawyers, bankers and other hangers on. All this in the name of free enterprise! Human folly is alive and well in management as it has always been only much more so.

It is, of course, all too easy to look back at what seemed like a golden age of the past or alternatively to look forward to a golden age in the future. Neither is realistic. Despite the cock-ups, modern management has implemented some remarkable projects just as our forefathers did.

In the UK the construction of terminal 5 at Heathrow or work on constructing the cross-rail link are each, in their own way, every bit as impressive as the design and construction of Crystal Palace. The technology used is

---

[i] *Bryan Burrough and John Helyar Barbarians at the Gate (London: Arrow Books) 1990.*

superior by orders of magnitude as is the way brainpower has often replaced brawn-power. Likewise, the coordination and the teamwork involved are also impressive. Each generation of management has its outstanding successes and failures and none is a golden age. The reality however is that despite our technology, science and business schools our management skills are no better and may even be worse than our ancestors.

Human nature is the same as it always was and although life for some may not be "nasty, brutish and short", the foibles of human nature are still very much the same in essence and behaviour as they always were.

The tasks and pitfalls of management have therefore hardly changed although the *nature* of management may be on the whole less coercive or hierarchical in the more affluent parts of the world. In the West we don't use slaves anymore and place much greater emphasis on the wellbeing and aspirations of employees although we do have zero hours contracts. There are few dark satanic mills in the West although sweatshops are still rife elsewhere. In advanced economies, work is much less about brawn and much more about brain. Even so it is doubtful if modern managers are more effective than those of previous generations. We may know more but we don't manage better. It is a chastening and sobering thought particularly for those who are tempted to believe ours is a golden age of enlightened management.

Fantasy or Reality?

Chapter 7 - Confusion Confounded

We trained hard but every time we were beginning to form up into teams, we would be re-organised. I was to learn later in life that we tend to meet any new situation by re-organising and a wonderful method it can be for creating the illusion of progress while producing inefficiency and demoralisation
- GAUIS PETRONIUS.

Managerial leadership is the bedrock of any successful company, institution or organisation. Since time immemorial there have always been those who led and organised and those who followed and were organised. We are talking about the managers and the managed, the leaders and the led, the tellers and the told.

This has never changed and human nature being what it is, there is little likelihood that it will ever change. Look around and you will see the desire of the few to lead and the willingness of the many to be led. It underwrites, for better or for worse, virtually every collective human endeavour and has always done so.

The purpose of managerial leadership is to make beneficial things happen. This means there should be no place in management for

    i.   The apathetic who never know what is happening.

    ii.   The bureaucrats whose idea of action is red tape.

    iii.   The passive who watch things happen.

    iv.   The daydreamers who are hopelessly impracticable.

v. The obstructive who try to stop anything happening.

vi. The theoreticians who endlessly debate what should or should not happen.

Managerial leaders succeed by motivating others 'to do and achieve'. Show me a failing organisation and I will show you a failing leader. Show me a successful one and I will show you a successful leader. Managerial Leaders get results by leading from the front. Leadership relies first and foremost on common sense. I have never met a successful manager who did not use commons sense. It is practical, pragmatic and hands-on and calls for a perceptive understanding of human nature. It emphasises clarity, simplicity and practicability. All this is second nature to a seasoned manager.

The importance of common sense and pragmatism needs to be shouted from the rooftops of all business schools. It should be hung on banners attached to their ivory towers although that is highly unlikely to happen. The trouble is, as Marcus Sieff who was the successful Chairman of Marks & Spencer between 1972 and 1984, wrote: '… it is often the simplest wisdom which is more difficult to find, and common sense is not commonly distributed'.[i] If only some of his much less successful successors, who nearly destroyed the company, had understood this.

---

i Marcus Sieff *Management the Marks & Spencer Way* (London: FONTANA/Collins 1991) ISBN 0-00-637448-4

Alas the pragmatic approach to management epitomised by Lord Sieff and other outstanding leaders, is in real danger of being abolished by the onslaught of management by theory. Confusion is being progressively confounded. People, leadership and common sense are not how the Management Myth Making Industry perceives management. It is instead more concerned with bureaucratic paperwork, complex computer systems, processes, structures, strategies, techniques and theories.

According to the blurb for one Harvard Business School programme some years ago, senior executives had to become 'architects of a profound industry transformation'.[ii] What on earth are those highfalutin words supposed to mean? It was apparently no longer enough for organisations to be 're-engineered, realigned and re-structured'[iii]. The truth of the matter is, of course, that the slogans 're-engineering, realignment and restructuring' far from being 'not enough' frequently did more harm than good. They were never, ever central to effective management. If anything they contributed to mismanagement.

The gurus in the ivory towers of Harvard and elsewhere talk airily about 'breaking the shackles of traditional management techniques'[iv] when sensible people were never shackled by them in the first place. They conveniently forget to mention that 'traditional

---

ii Harvard Business School. Prospectus for *"What's Next & So What? Leading in the 21st Century"*. (*www.exed.hbs.edu/programs/wnsw/index.html*)
iii ibid.
iv ibid

management techniques' were invented and sold by them in the first place. So their advice really is "don't do what we said yesterday, do what we say today and when that fails (as it will if our track record is any guide) do what we will say to-morrow. Oh, and by the way, don't forget to pay our large fees promptly as we need a healthy cash flow to finance our ivory towers, creature comforts and huge gross margins."

The real problem is not only *'What they don't teach you at Harvard Business School*[v] it is the hype they do teach. Too much is based on theoretical case studies some of which are positively misleading and/or based on such scant and/or selective research as to be risible. As the inimitable Peter Drucker once put it with incisive clarity: 'the Harvard elite are missing some pretty fundamental requirements for success:

i.   Humility

ii.   Respect for people on the firing line

iii.   Deep understanding of the nature of business and the kind of people who can enjoy themselves making it prosper

iv.   Respect from way down the line

v.   A demonstrated record of guts, industry, loyalty, judgement, fairness, and honesty under pressure.'[vi]

---

v Mark H McCormack *What They Don't Teach You at Harvard Business School* (London: Fontana/Collins) 1986. ISBN 0-00-636953-7
vi Robert Townsend *Up The Organization* (London: Coronet Books 1971 ISBN 0 340 14986 8 p 66

Business schools are not shy when it comes to boasting how much their graduates can expect to prosper. Their sales pitch is often mostly about the money its graduates can earn rather than about the learning. One MBA concluded 'business schools are, on anything but a personal level for their graduates, wasting time and resources.' As a member of the Association of MBA's, I used to receive its newsletters, which made a regular feature of notes from recent graduates evaluating their gains from courses. Almost without exception, the emphasis was on the highly paid jobs they had succeeded in getting because of their MBA's, not the merits of the courses themselves. Is this really what business schools are about – sky-high rewards to the business graduates - but financial disaster to the businesses and investors?[vii]

The success of the post-war economies of Japan and Germany, who did not have Business Schools, provides compelling evidence of how unimportant they are in reality. One staggering statistic about the Japanese economy says it all. Over a 30-year period, Japan sustained an average growth rate of 10% per annum. Until China took centre stage no good-sized economy in 6,000 years had approached anywhere near such an incredible rate for such a long period. The success of the German and Japanese economies had nothing to do with conventional business school theories or textbooks.

---

vii Brian Hershman in letter to <u>Oxford Today</u> (Volume 15 No 2 Hilary 2003) p 62

When the Japanese were busy decimating their foreign competitors in the 1970s and 1980s, those academics, consultants and gurus, who were not sat on the sidelines crying foul and unfair competition or looking for a sinister plot to turn into a conspiracy theory, were flocking to Japan in droves to see why they were so successful.

The truthful explanation Toyota[viii] gave for its success was simple: "we eliminate waste". This was far too prosaic for the Western intellectual mind. After all, how can you sell a management theory based on eliminating waste or persuade the Harvard Business Review to publish an article on, say, *The Strategy of Waste Management*? So the gurus packaged what they thought the Japanese did (or rather should in theory do) into sellable techniques such as 'Quality Circles', 'Kanban' and 'Just-in-Time' and earned a great deal peddling them. Twenty years later the pundits came much nearer to the reality when they started to talk about lean manufacturing methods. But why not simply concentrate, as the Japanese did, on eliminating waste of all kinds and not on inventing techniques with fancy sounding names?

Much to the chagrin of Toyota managers, western commentators turned what Toyota did on its head. Toyota perceived 90% of what they did as eliminating waste and 10% using techniques. Western gurus interpreted that as 90% technique and 10% eliminating waste. On one of my visits to Japan, as part of a study tour organised by a

---

viii Shigeo Shingo *Study of 'TOYOTA' Production System* (Tokyo: Japan Management Association). Third Printing 1982.

Management Consultancy Group, the focus was almost entirely on techniques such as Quality Circles as though they were the key to Japan's success.

Since Japanese and German industry prospered without business schools, it is hard to believe that the prosperity of the United States owes much, if anything, to the Management Myth Making Industry even though its home is in the USA. Indeed, it is arguable that US prosperity happened in spite of the theories. After all the US economy had a massive start on Japan and Germany after the war. It also has a lot of natural resources (Japan has none to speak of), its technological and global reach is far and away ahead of any other country and it has a remarkable 'can do' culture. Yes, it also has a lot of theories but why does it need them?

The culture of theory is such that even medium sized organisations are now frequently infested with fantasy - theories, models, methodologies, gobbledygook and incomprehensible memos circulated to all and sundry via electronic mail. They have hordes of consultants on lucrative rates crawling all over them like bees round a honey pot. It is all meetings, politicking, talk, expense account travel and very little 'doing'. Management through people has been replaced by mismanagement through bureaucracy, consultancy, paperwork *and* theory.

An American economist Leo Cherne observed, "The computer is incredibly fast, accurate, and stupid. Man is incredibly slow, inaccurate, and brilliant. The marriage of the two is a force beyond calculation." Unfortunately the marriage of a slightly different kind between theory and technology has created a gigantic paperwork bureaucracy and the frenetic compulsion of 24 - 7 emails that intrudes on the personal lives of many managerial leaders and staff. Even holidays are sometimes not sacrosanct. Research by O2 for 2014 suggests the average worker spends 36 days per year composing e-mails and workers in London send 4,000 and receive 6,000 emails a year.[ix]

The growth of the Management Myth Making Industry has unfortunately been accompanied by the growth of blatant and widespread corruption that brought the global financial industry to its knees in 2008-9 and is still rife in the financial sector today. My generation of managerial leaders find this wholly unbelievable. When I first started work as a manager there was a much greater sense of "right" and "wrong" in management than there is today. In our naivety we believed the job of a manager was to make a beneficial difference and we had some sense of social responsibility, albeit perhaps one that was too limited.

A cardinal concern of managerial leaders was to take more care with other people's money (particularly that of shareholders) than of their own. I once worked for a Managing Director who refused to allow his secretary to charge an electric plug for his use at his home to expenses, even though he owned a majority of the company's shares. Harold MacMillan, a former prime minister, used to relate how, in his family business, directors even paid for their

[ix] Cityam.com/2136658/email. 26th May 2015

personal postage stamps. Arnold Weinstock, Managing Director of GEC, who enjoyed the good life at his own expense outside the office, was scrooge like in his control of expenses at the office. He even stopped his Chairman, Lord Nelson, buying boating magazines on expenses much to the latter's chagrin. This kind of managerial integrity is now all too rare.

Too often nowadays, managers are perceived as being more concerned with lining their own pockets rather than contributing to the greater good and making a beneficial difference. They do this by means of share options, generous pension provisions, large expense accounts and the like, at the expense of shareholders, customers and fellow employees. It seems the real purpose of too many companies is now to enrich senior managers at the expense of customers, staff and shareholders.

Differentials in both pay and conditions between the leaders and the led are greater now than they have ever been. Today it is not regarded as incongruous or obscene, as it once was, to give managers large increases and pensions at the same time that mass redundancies are taking place and pension schemes for employees are being closed or restricted. In the army it is a cardinal principle that officers ensure other ranks eat before the officers do so. The reverse seems to now prevail in management. Nothing could be more divisive or conducive to bad management.

We at least used to *try* and pay managers by results, difficult as that was. It is now common practice to do the opposite. We pay fat cats at the top of the tree, in public and private sectors, huge sums for abject failure, crass stupidity and grubby machinations. A survey in the UK of management salaries found that 45% of "underperforming senior managers" received a bonus and that managerial salaries increased by more than inflation[x]. The more shareholders or public money they squander, the more some of them seem to get paid as an inducement to leave. This beggars belief and really is the nadir of managerial leadership.

There have, of course, always been "meals-on-wheels" managers whose main pre-occupations were wining and dining at the expense of shareholders. What was at one time a minority sport has mushroomed into corporate junkets held in luxury hotels, sometimes in foreign climes, with no expense spared. Such events are held "to build team spirit", "to celebrate and reward success" or whatever seems a good or plausible reason at the time. If it isn't, the attitude is too often 'so what, the shareholders are paying!' The main consideration is that neither facts nor integrity should stand in the way of spending shareholders, customer's or taxpayers' money. The corrosive free lunch syndrome is alive and well only more so!

The harmful effects of modern theories are nowhere more evident in the UK than in the National Health Service. At the end of 1970s, nurse training in the UK left the hospitals

[x] National Management Salary Survey 2015 (Chartered Management Institute)

where it was a success and subsequently headed into the universities where it was theorised. Apparently student nurses learn that altruistic caring is merely an example of the exploitation of women by a male-dominated medical profession. Student nurses are supposedly taught phenomenology, ethnography, economics reductionism and the rest of a range of post-modernist mumbo jumbo. What all this has to do with nursing (or what today is called the 'patient experience') is wholly beyond comprehension.

The powers-that-be seems to want to have fewer but larger regional hospitals and to run them like factories used to run but no longer do. This is presumably with the theory of economies of scale in mind. Instead of treating patients in one hospital visit, the patient (and their families) must make innumerable visits and experience long inbuilt delays and innumerable car parking fees. The system is strangled by queues and paperwork. You could not make it up!

The NHS always seems to have a serious shortage of nurses. Yet not that long ago it was insisting that any former nurse who wanted to return to nursing, after a period off for raising children, had to attend a thirty-week refresher course to update themselves. Most of the updating was apparently concerned with subjects such as the politics of health and had little to do with nursing practice or clinical skills.

Such crass stupidity is an unfortunate testimony to the influence and power of wrong-headed theories and theorists in management and contemporary society. No Minister of Health, or bureaucrat in the National Health Service, has had the grip, gumption, or guts to stop it. It has not even yet begun to dawn on the thickheaded political establishment that it is well nigh impossible to find a genius who can efficiently centrally manage an organisation employing 1.2 million people driven by political rather than clinical imperatives.

The worry is that this kind of mentality has spilt over to medical matters. A doctor told me recently that he too often had to do what the NHS laid down almost irrespective of the real needs of patients.

The results can be seen in any hospital in the UK. A few years ago my wife was admitted to Colchester General Hospital in Essex, England with a suspected heart condition. The quality of medical care, the concern and kindness were really excellent. Nonetheless the organisation of the then mixed ward was chaotic. According to the notice board they had care plans, team policies and all the meaningless paraphernalia, which the bureaucrats in the Health Service insist upon. None of these have anything whatsoever to do with medical treatment or the wellbeing of patients or good management.

No one seemed concerned at the hospital with the kind of essentials and leadership which old-fashioned matrons and ward sisters used to insist upon. The night staff spent a lot of their time talking thus keeping patients awake - something that would have never happened with earlier generations. One member of staff caused a commotion in the middle of the night by falling over a trolley in the dark that should never have been left where it was in the first place. The food was almost inedible and the levels of waste high.

The Institute of Health Care Management in the UK, which represents 10,000 professional staff, searched far and wide to find a way of improving the skills of NHS staff. One bright spark thought up a really good wheeze to boost confidence and build team spirit. So they employed Bosco, a freelance clown, to teach staff at £200 ($300) a head how to spin plates, walk tightropes and throw custard pies. Is it any wonder that the National Health Service in the UK is in such a shambles? Why they need to bring any more clowns in is a complete mystery.

The bureaucracy in the NHS knows no bounds. It insisted that a British citizen, the daughter of a doctor friend, who lived in the UK all her life but, who did her training to be a doctor as a mature student in Czechoslovakia, had to pass an examination in English before she was allowed to apply to sit a qualifying UK medical exam! They even refused to fix a date for the medical exam until she had taken and passed the totally unnecessary English examination. The process took a year. She then obtained a pre-registration post subsequently to be told later that the course she did in Czechoslovakia was so comprehensive that she was entitled to full registration immediately. This when there is a crying need for more doctors! It's pure bureaucratic madness!

No wonder a group of managers who examined the Health Service some years ago were so scathing about its management and organisation. They found the service has one administrator for every two clinical staff, that there were more administrators than beds and said too much money was being spent on bureaucracy. One chairman had an office the size of the casualty department. They alleged that managers exploited their positions to become 'fat cats' at the expense of patients and medical staff. By contrast, he entrances to the hospitals they visited were 'tatty, scruffy, dirty' and littered with cigarette ends.

No surprise either that a survey, conducted shortly after the managers study, found that at least a third of all the family doctors in the Health Service used the private sector for treatment of themselves and their families. Another more recent survey indicated that at least 20% of existing doctors were planning to retire early because of the bureaucracy, paperwork and stress.

Like the Health Service, Education in the UK has been similarly submerged in paperwork including curriculum plans, lesson plans, post-class warm and then cold feedback, reflection notes and others meaningless forms. Stressed teachers have to work long hours, not to teach, but to keep up with the paperwork. It is madness not management. Why the rest of us put up with the ministrations of the bureaucratic educational theorists is beyond my understanding. For six years I was a school governor and the amount of paper even we received was voluminous.

If sanity is to return to managerial leadership, we need to change the balance and use theory much less and pragmatism much more. At the end of the day what matters are favourable outcomes. To achieve these, organisations and their managers need to be freed from the shackles of political and managerial correctness. Confusion is confounded and compounded by indoctrination into unproven theoretical models and techniques that, worryingly, can provide an illusion of progress.

The what, why and how of using the alternative pragmatic and experiential approach to management is discussed in the next section.

Fantasy or Reality?

PART TWO: *REALITY*

So, What Should Be Done?

Fantasy or Reality?

Chapter 8 - See the Wood for the Trees

A fool sees not the same thing as a wise man sees
- WILLIAM BLAKE

Management is not a pleasant stroll in park. In some situations the pressures are so great that managerial leaders experience a sensory overload enveloping them in a fog of confusion. This prevents them from seeing the wood for the trees. When this happens managers are not clear where they are, where they want to go and how to get there. Their organization becomes rudderless and at the mercy of events, sometimes with serious or even disastrous consequences. The fog of management is every bit as real (and dangerous) as the fog of war.

Poor communications are endemic in such situations. We have all played the party game where a message is whispered to one person who whispers it to the next and so on along the communication chain of people. What comes out at the end is never the same as what went in at the beginning.

The fog mostly descends when managers are confronted with an accumulation of problems that are outside their experience (as described in chapter 3) or when they face a multiplicity of complex problems. My last major task before retiring from Digital was to lead a two-day meeting between major global customers and the senior executives of Digital. One was so stressed out that I suggested that instead of making a presentation he sat and chatted to customers, exchanged views and asked them what their problems were. He was too stressed to take in my advice and gave a presentation that hardly inspired customer confidence. He clearly could not see the wood for the trees.

He was suffering, like many managers do, from working long hours with a punishing schedule of meetings, world travel and trying to cope with a deteriorating business outlook he did not understand. He was imprisoned in a kind of executive bubble or an underground bunker with an incessant deluge of relevant and irrelevant information. Each day executives endure countless pressures in the form of emails, briefings, conflicting demands and opinions, reports, gossip, snippets, accounts, phone calls and. What's more, the bad news is too often sugar coated and good news exaggerated by well-meaning subordinates with no experiences of crises.

In a relatively stable or slowly changing environment managers lead and control their organisation by regular measurement and reporting cycles. They monitor performance and financial results provided by their management information system. The monthly information pack for a board meeting of even a medium-sized company is often inappropriately voluminous. Page upon page of detailed analysis presented every which way – gross margins, net margins, measured by products and by markets, cash flow, balance sheet, projections and umpteen other things.

When things go wrong, such data overload makes keeping a grip on reality very hard indeed. It is just as problematic as having a shortfall of useful up to date information. It means that managers need a lot of stamina, good sense and an ability to think the unthinkable. They don't have the 'luxury' of time to sit back and reflect. Managerial leaders in difficult circumstances need to be able to form a bird's eye view of what is happening and make clear decisions. In order to see the wood for the trees, managers need to sit on top of the information hierarchy and make their decisions based on bite-sized exception reporting.

One who was not a victim of data-overload was Arnold Weinstock. He used to control the GEC-Marconi group of companies from a small headquarters office at Stanhope Gate London. Weinstock had a remarkably small number of staff in relation to the size of the company. He had a reputation as a numbers manager with a photographic memory. Weinstock also possessed an uncanny ability to identify shortcomings and problems. Each managing director of his companies had a phone on his desk that only Weinstock could ring. When Weinstock appointed new MD's he told them the less that phone rang the better!

I had the privilege of meeting him once when I was exploring the possibility and opportunities of working for his group. I was astonished at his knowledge of the management personnel in his companies. I was like a fly on the wall when he and his group personnel manager candidly discussed where I could fit in and the strengths and weaknesses of those I could be working with. He was very shrewd indeed in his judgment of people and contrary to his public persona, he clearly did not manage purely by numbers.

The fog of management is also made worse by false optimism and self-deception. This is particularly so in larger organisations where managers can and do receive so much adulation they are almost portrayed as capable of walking on water. This dulls their thinking and perceptions and causes them to lose the plot. It happened to Ken Olsen in Digital who was regarded as virtually infallible. It did not seem to have happened to Steve Jobs in Apple who really was amazing but was far from a saint[i]. Most managerial leaders have to guard against hubris.

You cannot drive a car if you cannot see the road and you cannot drive well if overloaded with sensory data. This is the key problem manager leaders face. Harold MacMillan, when Chancellor of the Exchequer, claimed it was like having to run the economy with the equivalent of an out-dated copy of Bradshaw's railway timetables. This is exactly what managers' face - either incomplete out of date information or simply too much data. Each leads to confusion and uncertainty. It is also worth remembering that computers need data, humans need information. Computers also have lots of memory, but absolutely zero imagination!

Inadequate or misleading information is a major reason for not seeing the wood for the trees. According to a recent article, 16% of companies in the UK know of and admit to faults in their spreadsheets that consolidate their management information. The true numbers are certainly much larger. An analysis of 15,770 spreadsheets found 755

---

[i] *Walter Isaacson Steve Jobs (London: Little Brown 2011) ISBN 978-1-4087-0374-8*

files with more than a hundred errors. The maximum number of errors in one file was 83,273! British companies use spreadsheets in the preparations of accounts worth up to £1.9 trillion. The UK manufacturing sector uses spreadsheets to make pricing decisions for up to £170bn of business. Reports suggest that JP Morgan lost £250m because of a spreadsheet slip up in 2013. Axa Rosenberg, the global equity investment management company, was fined £150m for covering up a spreadsheet error.[ii]

For these reasons, effective managerial leaders use a variety of methods to develop their own formal and informal sources of information. They go beyond and behind the numbers to keep their feet on the ground and to distinguish the wood for the trees. They also ensure they look outwards and inwards.

Some use the kind of analysis and creativity used by Nicola Renshaw as described in Chapter 3. What she did was not rocket science. It was just a simple comparison of three readily available figures from three companies to estimate the extent to which Digital was hugely over staffed.

One of the first lessons I learnt in my first real managerial staff job as Personal Assistant to the Production Manager was the importance of systematically recording and analysing information. The management accounts measured what the results were. The production

---

[ii] *Daily Telegraph 7th April 2015. These findings are not new. Countless studies over the years have revealed the large number errors in spreadsheets.*

manager's own figures I provided and updated helped him to understand why.

Since then I have always used similar techniques. I have found using moving annual totals (MAT's) of a few key parameters helped me understand what was really happening in a variety of companies and situations. The insights I gained were amazing and certainly help me see beyond the fog. There are, of course, limitations to MAT's and like everything else they can be misleading but they were very much part of my managerial toolbox.

The point is that effective managers are always making mental or back of envelope calculations. They develop a multiplicity of information channels and analysis for making key judgements. They know the kinds of information they need for their business and have a kind of sixth-sense not to accept all information or numbers at the face value.

A manager needs to have a feel for numbers and their magnitude but not be mesmerised by them. Most of us understand what say one hundred means, some understand what one million means but larger sums become meaningless abstractions. This is partly why politicians get criticised for wasting a hundred thousand pounds but get away with squandering millions or even billions. In politics a million here, a million there is almost meaningless and seems like chicken feed. Politics is for the birds!

When I used to teach students and explained how to pass exams I used to show them how effective it is, mentally, to ask questions of an exam question to help formulate their answer. Successful managers do something very similar when they have to cut through a mass verbiage and sort the wheat from the chaff.

Wise managerial leaders understand the importance of bad news and always thank those who deliver it to them and are never ever rude to the messenger. They know that bad news can be a springboard not for a witch-hunt, as too often happens, but to improve how the organization operates to avoid similar bad news in future. Good news provides no incentive to improve and may even lead to the kind of complacency than can turn good news into bad news. Now that really is a paradox!

A similar consideration applies to whistle-blowers. Managers should encourage them because they reveal hidden abuses, problems and practices that are detrimental to efficiency and the wellbeing of an organisation. Instead the opposite too often happens. They close ranks to protect their reputation, hound the whistle-blowers and it is even not unknown for them to promote those whose actions caused the abuse.

In the UK, for years the National Health Service got away with their appalling persecution of whistle-blowers who were doing a public service in telling the truth.[iii] They isolate them and then spend a small fortune on lawyers to denigrate, intimidate and undermine them. They threaten legal action, put skilled and scarce medical practitioners on

---

[iii] *In fairness there is evidence the NHS culture is now changing for the better. It certainly needed to do so.*

long paid garden leave and use confidential clauses as part of settlements. They never hesitate from lying like troopers to conceal the truth, protect the guilty and to hide the wood for the trees. Incredibly the head of the body that oversaw the Mid Staffordshire Trust in its darkest days was actually made Head of the NHS. He presumably worked on the basis of "hear no evil, see no evil"!

One manager who usually saw the woods for the trees was the irascible and legendary Allen Clarke, who ran the Plessey Group in the immediate post war years. He drove his staff to distraction by getting "lost" and wheedling his way into factories unannounced to find out for himself what was going on. He really had his finger on the pulse of the organisation. Apparently he once saw someone who appeared to be doing nothing. He asked him how much he earned, fired him on the spot and in lieu of notice paid him off in cash from his own pocket. The individual concerned was actually a driver from another company waiting for his lorry to be loaded and did not at all mind the extra cash!

A protective mechanism some Managerial Leader use is 'truth tellers'. These are trusted confidants who are in a position to tell a leader he or she is wrong or is making a big mistake. The takes courage, discretion, and integrity while not becoming a yes man or woman. To do so is far from easy. It requires a strong relationship of mutual trust and respect between the leader and truth teller. Truth tellers perform a vital function in quietly and unobtrusively lubricating an organisation. By their nature they have a low visibility and often have an innocuous managerial tile that does not reflect the influence they exert. Savvy sales personnel instinctively understand that the key to a sale is to find and convince a customer's truth teller. They are often the silver fox in an organisation – the one who has a major influence - but never really outwardly appears to have.

I have known a few managers who keep their finger on the pulse by randomly inviting groups of managers and staff to join them for coffee or tea where they can raise anything they want. This kind of truth telling can be very effective but a manager in doing this has to be careful to ensure it is not a means of settling grievances or old scores. The manager needs to listen not promise.

From watching the UK TV series The Apprentice I would guess the truth tellers Lord Sugar greatly relied on were Margaret Mountford and Nick Hewer but I could be very wrong. Clinton Silver was probably the truth teller in Marks and Spencers[iv] when Rick Greenbury was in charge. In my own managerial career I have always been fortunate to have colleagues or subordinates who were truth tellers and usually managed, but not alas always, to restrain my wilder and foolish impulses and schemes. We all learn by making mistakes.

Seeing the wood for the trees can sometimes give an enormous competitive advantage. At Brighton Hill School in Basingstoke, where I was a governor, we realised from a simple analysis of feeder school numbers that there was

---

[iv] *Judi Bevan The Rise and Fall of Marks and Spencer (London: Profile Books 2002) ISBN 1 86197 431 0.*

going to be a large drop in the numbers entering secondary schools[v]. This would result in redundancies as money follows pupils. So we thought outside the box and took action to attract entrants from outside our catchment area. It was so successful that the school was over-subscribed and had to increase its capacity when other schools had to reduce theirs and make staff redundant with a loss of morale.

Any of the other secondary schools could have done what Brighton Hill did but it was outside the experience of their governors and managers. They had access to exactly the same information but they failed to connect the dots and see the trends. At the outset, Brighton Hill was not the best performing school in Basingstoke in terms of exam results. As staff morale, confidence and enthusiasm rose, engendered by success in attracting students, the school gradually climbed towards the top of the exam league table. Staff instead of being worried about their future, shaped their future. It really did pay to see the wood for the trees.

When management fails to see the wood for the trees they set a course for failure. Looking down into the abyss is very difficult but clutching at straws, hoping for the best or retreating to a dream world does not work. Whatever their managerial leadership style, managers need always to see the wood for the trees and face its truths however unpleasant. Not doing so sows the seeds of decline and

---

[v] Most managers in private sector companies would almost give their right arm for the accurate forecasts schools can make of future intakes.

failure. To sow the seeds of success managerial leaders have to understand and face up to reality and its consequences. There is no other option.

Fantasy or Reality?

Chapter 9 - Do the Right Thing

The supreme quality for leadership is unquestionably integrity. Without it, no real success is possible, no matter whether it is on a section gang, a football field, in an army, or in an office.
- DWIGHT D. EISENHOWER

Leadership is about having the courage and honesty to do the right thing, in the right way for the right reasons. It is about making courageous choices instead of convenient ones. Leadership is also not about popularity but about what is right. Effective leaders make decisions based on their sense of values and integrity in order to benefit the entire organisation.

Unfortunately, in today's world of guru inspired 'management speak' we too easily lose sight of this simple truth. Facts are rarely allowed to speak for themselves but instead are wrapped in hype. The context is too often now more important than the content. Gloss and spin are everything and everywhere in virtually all aspects of management. It is distinctly unfashionable to call a spade a spade when it can be described as a 'implement for digging holes'.

What is true is that the level of trust has gradually declined across a wide spectrum. Banks were once highly regarded as truthful, honest and upright. After their mis-selling, money laundering, the sheer greed of their executives and traders, the cheating in fixing Libor rates, the way they treat customers plus the machinations and sheer incompetence that led to the financial meltdown in 2008 who, with an atom of sense, now trust them?

The same is true of journalists. They act as though they have a God given right to intrude on personal matters; hack phones; harass, chase and photograph individuals using motorcycles. Then they slant their reporting in accordance with the prejudices of the proprietors; emphasise salacious gossip; and act virtually as a Fifth Estate who are above and beyond the law. They do this in the guise of freedom. Isn't it staggering how the media moguls' waltz in and out of Downing Street seemingly at will? Even quality papers such as The Times rarely now provide a straight factual account of what has happened but mix in comment. The one exception is probably the New York Times that has a reputation for straight reporting.

I once had an article published in the Financial Times. Even the business editor said I ought to add colour to my first paragraph to attract the reader. In naivety I replied "but I thought the FT was coloured pink"! After amending the first paragraph I was, however, very impressed indeed at the way in which he carefully checked every statement and detail to ensure it was both correct and clear. It gave me confidence in the integrity of the FT, which I retain to this day.

The roll call of what Churchill once described as terminological in-exactitudes is already very long and growing and is almost on par with the Management Myth Making Industry. One would think the Financial Sector would learn but it does not do so and continues to transgress almost with impunity. Few rogue financiers go to prison in the UK although a higher proportion do in the

USA. No one trusts politicians and with good reason. Few trust insurance companies. Financial and other scams are widespread. Multinationals like Apple are virtually beyond national tax laws. Even churches have sought to cover up criminal abuses by some of their priests and others. Whereas it was commonplace to trust, it is sadly now commonplace to distrust.

The corrosive effects of distrust between organisations and enterprises and within them are enormous. At one time a deal was sealed with a handshake. Not anymore. The litigious climate in the US has invaded the western world. In the UK it used to be unusual to have a chief legal officer on the board except for large multinational companies. Now it is common practice in subsidiaries of US companies and many others as well. Terms and conditions and long-winded legal contracts are now the order of the day. Even governments have to be very careful to avoid being sued by the giant American monoliths. We used to have a tradition that a man's word was his bond!

The effect on management is devastating because Managerial Leaders if they are to succeed *have* to do the right thing. They have to be fair and honest in dealing with staff and do what is right when taking *major* decisions. Leadership is not about popularity but it is about trust. The leader does not necessarily win friends but has nevertheless to influence people. Leadership is by its nature a very lonely task. It can be particularly so when a manager feels the need to step out of line.

This happened to me early in my management career in Philips. I faced two dilemmas when I did what I thought was the right thing even though in one case it could have had a harmful effect on my future.

The first arose when Philips took in a controlling interest in Pye and there was some rationalisation between the two companies. Pye companies, that were smaller and much more entrepreneurial than their staid Philips counterparts, sought not unreasonably to gain benefits from being in the Philips group. Pye Cathodeon Crystals wanted the advanced computer design software for filters that one of my groups had developed over the years. I refused to allow them access because I thought they would become a competitor. This was not the kind of stand other managers had taken but I thought it the right thing to do.

When Mr Tromp, the number 2 in the worldwide Phillips hierarchy, came to MEL on his final kind of state-visit before his retirement he asked 'where is Moyes?' He instructed me to sit next to him and over lunch berated me for not co-operating with Cathodeon. He did not take kindly when I replied it was his fault because the Board of Management had instructed we should work with Pye companies on a commercial and arm's length basis! I was finally so exasperated that I retorted: "you are only angry because your son-in-law is working for Cathodeon!" There was a horrified silence at my comment and even Tromp was speechless. Subordinates simply did not speak to the great man like that. Fortunately he was a generous man and when taking him round the factory afterwards he ruefully remarked "we could do with managers like you in Holland"!

At his last meeting of the Philips Board of Management he did however persuaded his colleagues to rescind the arms-length directive. Even so as he was retiring Cathodeon somehow did not get the access they wanted to our computer aided design software. Nelson was not the only managerial leader to understand the need to put a telescope to a blind eye although my eyesight in both eyes was perfectly good and I did not have a telescope!

Pye was the source later of another problem where I had once again to do what I believed was right. To prepare for the production of 'Clansman', a radio transmitter for the army, my company had to select and buy Automatic Test Equipment (ATE) financed by the Ministry of Defence. Three British suppliers put in tenders for the order. Two of the suppliers, had a good record of supplying such start-of-the art equipment and quoted prices considerably more than that quoted by a Pye company who had no experience in the field.

The price the Pye Company quoted was almost certainly below cost but on paper their tender ostensibly met the specifications. That meant there were no technical grounds to disqualify it. It seemed Pye either wanted to buy the business as a way into the market or possibly they thought they would be able to jack the price up once they got the order. This was not exactly unknown for Ministry of Defence (MOD) contracts in those days and it may not have changed much since!

Neither the Design Group at MEL who was responsible for the specification and purchase, or the technical staff in the MOD who had to approve the purchase wanted to take what was clearly a massive risk and opt for the lower priced Pye offer. Normally they would have found some means to reject the lowest cost tender. In this case they had to contend with the unwanted complication that the Chairman of Pye was Lord Thorneycroft who had been a Secretary of State for Defence and a Chancellor of the Exchequer.

His Lordship put considerable pressure on the MOD to secure the order for Pye via his contacts in the Cabinet and elsewhere and also via the Philips chain of management. As a consequence no one in either MOD or MEL was prepared to step out of line and take the right decision. The matter just dragged on and on from indecision to indecision.

As Production Manager the procurement was not in any way my responsibility but as one of my production units would be the user of the equipment and I realised that unless a decision was taken soon the equipment would be late and production would be delayed when all hell would be let loose.

After considering the options, Ken Foy (my production group manager for radio) and I decided the only way out of the impasse was to buy from Hewlett Packard (HP) who had been excluded from the original tender list because they were not British. They were, however, leaders in ATE and supplied much of the equipment any ATE supplier would use in their systems. HP had an excellent reputation for high quality equipment and customer service but tended to be highly priced.

So although it was theoretically nothing to do with me and I was, to put it mildly, greatly exceeding my authority, I gave John Pink of HP a copy of the tender document, told him I wanted a fully compliant proposal within two weeks (a tough call to meet) and also told him what the price needed to be. This was based on the lower one of the highest two prices with a small amount knocked off.

On receipt of HP's technically compliant proposal I took it to my Managing Director Richard Rankin and said, "Something needs to be done to break the impasse and the best way to do so is to go to HP." To his credit he supported me. The MOD thankfully accepted the decision as it got them off the hook as they could always blame MEL. His Lordship's bite proved less than his bark when faced with a 'fait accompli.'

John Pink and his boss David Baldwin (who later became Managing Director of Hewlett Packard in the UK) must have been surprised to get the order and probably never got an easier order in their careers. That said I am sure David was not entirely happy at the price or margin. In a truly open tender they would have probably got a higher price but I needed to ensure there would not be a price issue. Doing the right think again!

Preparing tenders of this kind is expensive and my actions were unfair to the two bona-fide suppliers but given the circumstances what other option was there? To give in to

Pye would have been totally wrong. Re-tendering was not an option since the tenders were technically compliant plus there was not the time or procedures in place for doing so. Managerial Leaders sometimes have to make moral decisions involving shades of grey and take actions they would prefer not to take. They have to do what they believe is right even when right is the least of the evils as it was in this case.

Doing what is right is not necessarily the same as doing what is best. It may, for instance, be right and decent for a company to voluntarily pay compensation, but that may not be the best for profits.

Personal integrity in management is also important for a purely practical reason. Despite the adulation they receive, Managers have to be brutally honest with themselves if they are to keep their feet on the ground. Nothing is more important in a manager than introspection and private self-doubt. They have, for example, to recognise when success is due more to fortuitous circumstances, as it often is, than to the efforts of their staff and themselves. I never cease to be amazed at the capacity of humans to claim credit for fortuitous successes, to which they had contributed nothing. Such claims ultimately end in tears because they are based on self-deception. When managers delude themselves and believe their own propaganda they plant the seeds for failure. This is clearly the wrong thing to do.

Humility is an important characteristic of the personal integrity of a leader in doing the right thing. According to

Dwight D Eisenhower 'A sense of humility is a quality I have observed in every leader who I have deeply admired. I have seen Winston Churchill with humble tears of gratitude on his cheeks as he thanked people for their help to Britain and the Allied cause. My own conviction is that every leader should have enough humility to accept, publicly, the responsibility for the mistakes of his subordinates he has selected and, likewise, to give them credit, publicly, for their triumphs.'[i]

Walking tall and taking personal responsibility is essential in a leader. Too many modern so-called managers seem intent on passing the buck elsewhere. 'Was none who would be foremost, to lead such dire attack: But those who cried 'Forward', And those who cried 'Back.''[ii] They should learn from General Eisenhower who before the landings in Europe in the Second World War prepared a press release, unknown even to his staff, taking all the blame if the landings failed. Would that some of the panjandrums and potentates at the top of our monolithic global enterprises and particularly banks emulate him.

Some would-be managerial leaders fail at the first crucial hurdle when they are given charge of others, yet progress up the tree because their managers thought it kind not to hurt them. Personal tragedy later results when a manager of long standing is suddenly told he or she is not up to the

---

[i] *John Adair Effective Leadership (London: Pan Books 1983) Churchill's humility did not extend to the public cut-and-thrust of politics. He described one opponent Ramsay MacDonald as "a boneless wonder" and his ex-wartime colleague Clement Attlee as "a modest man who has much to be modest about"! Outside the public arena he appears to have been kindly and generous.*
[ii] *Thomas Macaulay Lays of Ancient Rome*

job and is asked or told to leave. It happens much too often and the task of bearing the bad news to a middle-aged manager is one of the most unpleasant duties for a manager. Often the deficiencies have been obvious for years but out of consideration no one had ever done anything about them. Sparing feelings or avoiding confrontation is not kindness. Moral cowardice has no place in leadership; doing the right thing has.

One of the problems is that it is all too easy in management to become de-sensitised and forget that the job is about dealing with human beings. It must be very difficult for military leaders who know that their decisions, however good, will mean the loss of lives and dreadful suffering. Trying to strike a balance between being over sensitive or dehumanised must be particularly agonising.

At a personal level it is particularly difficult to take a decision about a close colleague. Managers fail like everyone else. They sometimes fail for reasons outside their control or sometimes because their environment has changed and they have not changed with it. They often fail because they have been promoted beyond their abilities. It is not easy to tell a subordinated manager, who is also a colleague and perhaps a friend that he or she has to leave the organisation. That is why sensible managers keep a distance between themselves and their subordinates and don't employ personal friends.

Too many of us have unfortunately seen or suffered from a lack of integrity in managers who did not do the right thing. In one company I knew the petty minded and vindictive directors promoted someone, who was probably psychopathic and certainly inadequate, to do their dirty work and rid the company of a number of really able and exceptional managers who had made a huge contribution to their company's prosperity – and the directors' own financial wellbeing. The harm he did was immense. He was of course rewarded – by being sacked. "Those who live by the sword, die by the sword" but alas not those who let him loose in the first place.

Bullies and cheats who have no regard for what is right sometimes manoeuvre themselves to the top of management and put their own best personal interests first. This happened for example at Enron, at a number of banks and in earlier times, the Maxwell organisation. They were built and sustained on the shifting sands of deceit and inevitably failed with disastrous consequences, some long lasting. Goldman Sachs, who for a large fee allegedly helped Greece falsify their national accounts to enter the Euro, is still a prosperous company. Crime may not pay but finance chicanery obviously does pay.

Only those who have agonised about a decision, which they know, will hurt a close colleague or a section of the work force can really understand how difficult it can be to do the right thing. I write as one who has made such decisions and also been at the receiving end of them. Either way the hurt is hard to bear.

Managerial Leadership is not an easy option and the temptations to fudge an issue, go with the flow or take a short cut are each seductively easy. Management is always difficult enough without adding further complications. Puritanism and management are not synonymous but at the end of the day taking the easy way out does not solve anything. There really is no option. Managerial leaders need the personal courage and integrity do what they believe is right. There is no place for cowardice in managerial leadership. The right decisions, however difficult, have to be made and even though the consequences are not universally popular. Doing what is right is the very essence of effective managerial leadership.

Chapter 10 - Think to Do

There are no whole truths; all truths are half-truths. It is trying to treat them as whole truths that plays the devil.
A. N. WHITEHEAD – philosopher and mathematician

One day my boss at Multitone Electric Ltd asked me to his office to talk about a new policy he wanted to implement. In his logical and precise Germanic manner he set out his basic premise and from this he explained, step-by-step in excruciating detail, the conclusions he had reached. At the end of an exhausting session for me he said triumphantly "there you are Peter this is what we should do."

When I disagreed my boss was flabbergasted and with hindsight I can't say I blame him. In his eyes logic was logic was logic. In my eyes logic was a fragile tool and there were limits to rationality. Although his logic and decision premise seemed impeccable to him, his conclusions did not *feel* right to me intuitively. We simply had different perceptions. He was mollified but bemused when I blandly explained, "you and I don't think alike".

What the eventual outcome was I don't remember. We probably creatively combined our two approaches into a modified agreed course of action neither of us had thought of before. I still vividly remember the conversation because as a result, it dawned on me that different people do think in different ways and that all our truths are really only perceptions. His approach was predominantly analytical, logical and precise; mine was predominantly creative, imprecise and intuitive.

We all seek our own truths in our own ways and none of us are ever completely right or wrong. What matters in management is being approximately 'right' - at least six times out of ten on key issues and policies. Judged by personal financial outcomes, my boss was much better in seeking his truths than I was in seeking mine since he retired a multi-millionaire. There is no justice in this world!

Although each manager's mind works differently, there is nevertheless a commonality in all-managerial thinking. It is ultimately a process of *synthesis* rather than *analysis*. Synthesis is the common denominator in translating ideas and knowledge in the mind into action in the real world.

A synthesis is not a grand or grandiose design. These are doomed to failure from the outset as they are merely the theoretical illusions of intellectual grandeur. None of us are immune from such illusions but practical management is about thinking through how to get things done in the real world and avoiding seductive illusions from cloud-cuckoo land.

Synthesis goes beyond data and logic. It uses common sense, judgement and wisdom. It relies on intuition, draws on experience, un-verbalised clues, gossip, even hunches. It is practical and based on a shrewd understanding of human nature. It is about analysing, conceiving, crystallising, designing, discovering, distilling, dreaming, experiencing, formulating, puzzling and sensing. One American company's motto is: 'Facts are available to everyone: intuition is proprietary'. It is so true.

It is the practical nature of turning knowledge and thinking into action that eludes many unsuccessful managers. Some find it difficult to translate thinking into doing even though they have the knowledge. Some always think they need that little bit more information before they can decide but never succeed in doing so. It is always easier to find reasons for doing nothing than doing something.

A common misconception is to assume 'thinking to do' is a kind of static or theoretical set-piece process. In some ways it resembles the process of climbing a mountain. When approaching the mountain the climbers first see the foothills. Then they climb the foothills and see further hills. They climb them and then see more hills. The process goes on until they actually see the mountain. In thinking terms the mind is continuously interacting with the changing nature of the environment.

Some academics and most consultants mostly think in *analytical* terms. As the eminent logician and philosopher, A J Ayer, ruefully confessed, 'It seems I have spent my entire life trying to make life more rational and it was all wasted effort'[i]. For academics, the intellect is the be-all-and-end-all. For managers, the intellect is simply part of the means of deciding what should be done.

The mechanistic inference that good decisions depend purely on adequate and accurate data plus analysis and penetrating intellect is naïve. If that were the case decisions

---

[i] *The Observer (17 August 1986)*

could be left to mechanistically intelligent computers and computer programmers. Perish the thought!

One of my colleagues in Digital, Russell Hart, found a decision making computer software application. He was so impressed by it that he wrote a review, which was published in Personal Computer World. He used the programme to choose his next company car. The choice it made, however, was not one Russell liked so he changed his original parameters to get the answer he wanted! Decisions in management always contain a subjective and judgemental element as Russell learnt.

Important managerial decisions (including the choice of a company car!) always involve dilemmas[ii], paradoxes, uncertainties and risks and calls for judgement and wisdom. If a manager did the impossible and digested all the works of all the leading management theorists and had all the market and other relevant information within his or her grasp, the manager would still not have the answers. That's because there are no answers in management only relevant questions.

Mental agility is sometimes, but not always, the hallmark of an excellent managerial leader. Yet there are many highly intelligent people who are hapless and hopeless managers and see the world in over complex terms. I know of a CEO of a large multi-national who had apparently everything going for him. He was singularly gifted: highly intelligent; a graduate of one of the world's top business

[ii]- *For the importance of dilemmas see Charles Hampden-Turner Charting the Corporate Mind (Oxford: Basil Blackwell 1990) ISBN 0-631-17735-3*

schools; multilingual; charming and charismatic; respected by men; admired by women and thought of as an all-round nice person. Still it literally took him nearly three (boring) hours to try to explain planned organisational changes.

As the Chinese philosopher Lao Tzu wrote in *Tao Te Ching* (How Things Happen): 'People who see the world in terms of theories often have a very intricate view of what is happening. Clarity is difficult for then. They are very hard to work with.' How true and how wise!

Anyone who entertains the notion that intellect alone is the passport to managerial success should read about Long-term Capital Management. The founders were mega-powered academics, including a Nobel Prize Winner. They believed they could beat the market and create unlimited wealth for themselves and their partners. Instead they created a trillion-dollar hole in the international banking system and almost caused it to crash. What's more, they got away with it, presumably on the basis that if you owe the bank some money you can't repay, you have a problem but if you owe the bank a mega amount you can't repay the bank has a problem![iii]

Enron prided itself on recruiting the intellectual crème-de-la-crème. Its chief executive was ex-McKinsey and Enron was nicknamed 'the house McKinsey built'. Enron deservedly came to a sticky end. It became clear that some of the 'crème-de-la-crème were nothing more than

---

[iii] *Roger Lowenstein When Genius Failed (London: Fourth Estate 2002). ISBN 1-84115-504-7*

intelligent crooks who perpetuated a huge accountancy swindle.

Although Enron paid about $10 million in annual fees to McKinsey in the years just before the meltdown, Rajat Gupta, the managing director of McKinsey at the time claimed its consultants did not "do anything that is related to any of the issues that got them into trouble"[iv]. But then he would, wouldn't he? There are none so blind as those who do not want to see!

Too much thinking in the British Civil Service is intellectual theorising. I found this out when I was appointed as one of three non-executive Directors of Data Recording Instruments charged with helping to privatise the state owned company. We received a mountain of papers with no less than seven different and detailed scenarios prepared for Ministers about what DRI should do. The excellent executives at DRI had spent far too much time supplying information so that Civil Servants could prepare even more scenarios. The whole thing was an absurd, circular paper chain and a waste of the executives' time.

A book by Jeffrey Pfeffer and Robert I Sutton[v] sought 'to understand why so many managers know so much about organisational performance, say so many smart things and work so hard, yet are trapped in firms that do so many

---

[iv] Quoted in _The Sunday Telegraph_ 2nd March 2003

[v] Jeffrey Pfeffer and Robert I Sutton _The Knowing-Doing Gap – How Smart Companies Turn Knowledge into Action (Boston: Harvard Business School Press 2000) ISBN 1-57851-124-0 p i et al_

things they know will undermine performance'. They found that 'many people knew what to do, but didn't do it'. They also pointed out: 'There is only a loose and imperfect relationship between knowing what to do and the ability to act on that knowledge.'[vi]

Those who 'think to do' have an aptitude for doing, those who don't have different aptitudes. It sounds this simple because it is this simple. People are different and have different aptitudes and skills. There is nothing wrong in that. As argued earlier, different minds and different personalities work in different ways and therefore excel at different things.

In my first job - as a radio and television service engineer - there was a gap between the aptitudes of practical doers and impracticable theorists. One type knew loads of theory but could not apply it. Another type did not really understand the theory and worked by rote, experience and guesses. The third type (of whom I was one!) had a good grasp of theory and crucially could apply the theories in practice.

The City & Guilds Institute had examinations for radio and television service engineers with a paper on theory and a practical test in fault finding. The pass rates for theory were high but low for the practical test. In one year, 76% of the candidates who passed the radio theory papers failed the practical test.

[vi] *ibid p 25*

Fantasy or Reality?

Theorising in management has become almost an end in itself and has obscured the central reality that management is about action. There is a widespread misconception in modern society that by talking about theories this equates to implementation. This ignores the fact that decisiveness and the 'bottom-line' is what makes a good manager. 'You can use the fanciest computers to gather the numbers, but in the end you have to set a timetable and act'.[vii]

Pfeffer and Sutton were wrong in supposing management is about translating theoretical knowledge into action. Managers don't normally start with knowledge and ask themselves "how can we use it?" They look at *what* they need to do and *why* and ask themselves *how*. Good managers think at the level of *awareness* rather than at the level of *knowledge*. The knowledge of a manager is simply one of the many aspects factored into the synthesis upon which 'thinking to do' decisions are made. What is crucial is having the wisdom to identify *relevant* knowledge, as distinct from theoretical knowledge, and to know how and when to use it.

In the welter of confusion between the practical and the academic, managers sometimes appear to be anti-intellectual. Many intellectuals look down on business leaders as philistine or predatory, or both '.[viii] Keynes described them as: 'Practical men, who believe themselves to be quite exempt from intellectual influences, are usually

[vii] *Lee Iaccora former CEO of Chrysler.*
[viii] *Marcus Sieff Management the Marks & Spencer Way (London: FONTANA/Collins 1991) ISBN 0-00-637448-4 p7*

the slaves of some defunct economist.'[ix] My perception is that Keynes tended towards intellectual arrogance.

This age-old divide between the intellectual and the practical, between academic sense and common sense, goes back to the Greek Philosophers. Plato wanted a special breed of 'super intellects' put in charge of everything to be known as 'philosopher kings'. Plato did not realise that philosophers are as flawed as all other human beings, or that throughout the course of history, many kings would prove to have feet of clay and be cruel tyrants.

Aristotle thought there were five intellectual virtues[x]:

1. *Sophia* – wisdom from understanding first principles:
2. *Episteme* – knowledge of discoverable facts;
3. *Phronesis* – prudence or judgement;
4. *Techne* – skill or art; and
5. *Nous* – intuitive reason or pure intelligence.

The father of philosophy believed *Sophia* was the most important since it dealt with the eternal and unchangeable.

If Aristotle's distinctions are valid then the combination of *sophia* (wisdom), *nous* (intuitive reason) and *episteme* (knowledge) correspond with the academic intelligence of the scholarly intellectual. These are not though, the kind of intelligence needed for successful management. The

---

[ix] *John Maynard Keynes General Theory of Employment, Interest and Money*
[x] *See article "A Question of Intelligence" by Paul Vallely in* The Independent *Friday 10th May 2002.*

practical intelligence a manager or leader needs consists more of *phronesis* (judgement), *techne* (skill) and *episteme* (knowledge) plus *nous* but with its modern common sense connotation.

There are two broad approaches managers use in thinking to do: *systemic* and *systematic*[xi]. The systemic right brain approach is predominately the way managers reach a synthesis. The systematic left-brain approach is the way they mainly analyse a problem. No approach is purely systematic (left brain) or purely systemic (right brain) and each approach contains elements of the other.[xii]

THINKING TO DO

SYSTEMATIC APPROACH	SYSTEMIC APPROACH
1. Looks for a method and makes a plan for solving a problem.	1. Keeps the overall issues/problems/objectives continually in mind.
2. Emphasises the process.	2. Frequently re-defines or re-frames the problem or issue.
3. Defends 'solution' in terms of the method. If the process is 'right' the outcome must be right.	3. Relies on intuition— unverbalised clues, even hunches
4. Defines the specific constraints early in the process.	4. Defends 'solution' in terms of 'fit'.
5. Works from the general to the specific in a process which increasingly refines the analysis.	5. Considers a number of options or alternatives simultaneously.
6. Uses and adhere to discrete steps and works in a reductionist way to a 'solution'.	6. Jumps from one step in analysis or searches for another and moves back again.
	7. Quickly explores and abandons alternatives.

[xi] *The table is not original thinking on my part. It may have originated from Jan Koolhas who was a colleague in Digital but I am not sure. My apologies for a lack of proper attribution*

[xii] *This is my subjective opinion resulting from experience and observation. I doubt if it can be proved or disproved.*

There is also another kind of divide in thinking apparent in managers. In a brilliant and fascinating philosophical essay[xiii], Isaiah Berlin quoted a line from a remaining fragment of the Greek poet Archilochus: 'The fox knows many things, but the hedgehog knows one big thing'. He thought there was a sense in which people were either fox like or hedgehog like in intellect.

Another view, from Oliver Wendell-Holmes, is that "There are one-storey intellects, two-storey intellects and three storey intellects with skylines. All fact-collectors, who have no aim beyond their facts, are one-storey men. Two-storey men compare, reason, generalise using the labours of fact-collectors as well as their own. Some second rank academics seem to have two-storey minds. Three-storey men idealise, imagine, predict; their best illuminations come from above, through the skylight'.[xiv] Successful managers are undoubtedly three-storey.

Whatever combination of thinking, systematic or systemic, hedgehog or fox, one-story, two-story, three-story, or an amalgam of them all, 'thinking to do' is hard work. It is also uncomfortable and unsettling, as the mind tends not to work office hours. Answers and actions don't spring out of nowhere and reaching them is as much sub-conscious as conscious.

[xiii] *Isaiah Berlin The Hedgehog and the Fox This was published as a separate booklet. It is also contained in Isaiah Berlin Russian Thinkers edited by Henry Hardy and Aileen Kelly (London: The Hogarth Press 1978) p 22 –82. ISBN 0-7012-0438-9*

[xiv] *Oliver Wendell Homes Jn the American writer Quoted by Stuart Crainer in The Ultimate Book of Business Quotations (Oxford: Capstone 1997). ISBN 1-900961-29-6.*

At a conscious level we reflect on an issue or problem in a number of different ways. We put the issue or problem to the back of our minds to the sub-conscious, and churn it over knowing that an answer or way of finding an answer will emerge. This is not mysticism. In everyday language we all use expressions such as "I will think about it" or "I will sleep on it". The most famous example of an answer emerging was when Archimedes stepped into his bath and saw the water overflow. He had the 'eureka' insight that led to the formulation of the law of fluid displacement. He used his discovery to prove that the goldsmith to the king of Syracuse had adulterated a gold crown with silver.

According to the film *The Dam Busters* the answer to the problem of flying aircraft at an exact height over a lake was solved when a member of the team attending a variety show. He noticed two converging spot lights and realised that adding two spotlights to the aircraft provided the answer.

In both these cases the mind was struggling with a major problem or rather formulating the right question(s). Questions play a key role in the mind of the manager. The philosopher Gilbert Ryle claimed 'Genius shows itself not so much as in the discovery of new answers as in the discovery of new questions.' Formulating the right question(s) is always in my experience the key to success in decision thinking.

When there are apparently insoluble issues or problems, managerial or technical, one of the biggest obstacle to a solution is the obvious that is kind of mental prison. We also too readily assume what is obvious to one person is not equally obvious to someone else. As a result we take the obvious for granted instead of challenging it in our thinking.

The mind always needs *elapsed* time to deal with a complex question or issue. The modern, politically correct craze for instant decisions is madness. No one can say, "I am going to be wise today" or "I am now going to spend time thinking about this issue". Human beings are simply not made like that. Decisions germinate in the mind of the manager: they are not produced like sausages. A manager frequently has to turn a problem over in his or her mind. The hallmark of the really good managerial decision maker is one who can say "I am not ready to make a decision on this issue". To say "wait" or "not yet" is much harder than saying "yes" or "no".

There are, of course, situations such as in a battle (or on a TV quiz show!) when people have to think on their feet and make decisions instantaneously. When there is fire there isn't the time to use a decision tree or debate whether to send for the fire brigade by first or second-class post! Good managers are decisive when they need to be decisive. Knowing when they need to be decisive is one of the arts of management and managerial thinking.

Those, such as military officers, whose job entails rapid decision making often spend a great deal of time beforehand in learning, preparing and training. No one becomes a military officer overnight without a great deal of training and practice. Those who are good at taking reflex decisions need to have good reflexes! And while management is always about action and not for those who stand and stare, it only rarely needs knee jerk reactions. Very few, if any, senior managers ever have to take a crucial decision in so short a time span with uncertain information. Fools rush in where managers should fear to tread. Making haste slowly is a wise precept in managerial thinking and decision-making. It is the action that needs to be quick and decisive once the decision is made.

Reflective thinking in management is mulling over what the manager already knows, factoring in experience and adding new relevant information. It is about using judgement and wisdom, making it into a coherent and workable synthesis and relating it to the problems and pressure faced. It commonly includes an element of realpolitik – a trade-off between what is ideal and what is possible. Letting the best be the enemy of the good is rarely sensible.

Academic thinking on the other hand does not have such managerial constraints. It is done in the pursuit of an objective and verifiable truth in science and something less in the arts. The difference between academic thinking and managerial thinking is illustrated by the contrast in their approaches to motivation by Maslow (an academic) and Robert Townsend (a practical executive). Maslow believed human beings have hierarchy of needs. This ranges from basic needs such as food and shelter at the bottom to self-actualisation at the top.

Townsend said we know this about man:

Think to Do

1. *He is a wanting animal.*
2. *His behaviour is determined by unsatisfied needs that he wants to satisfy.*
3. *His needs form a value hierarchy that is internal, not external:*
   (a) *Body (I can't breathe.)*
   (b) *Safety (How can I protect myself from …?)*
   (c) *Social (I want to belong.)*
   (d) *Ego (1. Gee, I'm terrific. 2. Aren't I? Yes)*
   (e) *Development (Gee, I'm better than I was last year.)*[xv]

Practical managers think and work at the Townsend summary level. Some may even prefer the more succinct and metaphorical language of the Bible, 'Man shall not live by bread alone…'[xvi]

Often serendipity plays a vital part in managerial thinking. If ever I made even a single numerical error in a report for my first boss at MEL, he immediately spotted it as if by magic. As I progressed in management I found I had the same kind of serendipity. Walking round a factory I would pick out the one faulty component in the only tray containing a faulty component.

Serendipity manifests itself in all kinds of ways. When I had nearly finished this chapter I saw a television programme about the Second World War and used the

---

[xv] *Robert Townsend Up The Organization – How to stop the company stifling people and strangling profits (London: Coronet Books 1971) ISBN 0 340 14986 8 p 127.*
[xvi] *Mathew iii.3 The Holly Bible*

information I learned about mulberry harbours to illustrate a point about clarity in decision thinking and taking.

Winston Churchill must rank as one of the clearest minded leaders ever. His decisions were crisp and clear. One of his most brilliant decisions in the Second World War was to decide, in face of considerable opposition and scepticism, on the building of two floating mulberry harbours each as big as Dover harbour. Churchill clearly understood, as a result of the raid on Dieppe, the difficulty if not impossibility of capturing an enemy port intact. So Churchill issued this brilliant instruction: 'Don't argue the matter, the difficulties will argue for themselves'. What superb leadership and thinking.

Clarity of the kind Churchill achieved is rare and hard to achieve but it is the essence of good decision thinking and making and is a model for all leaders and aspirant leaders.

Relevance is crucial in decision thinking. Managers must always be seeking for the *relevant* truth for the purpose they have in mind, as it is impossible to even begin to comprehend the truth of an organisation in all its complexity and richness. Management thinking is about knowing we cannot know but nonetheless, formulating a workable hypothesis.

This ability to instinctively pick out relevant information and truths is something I have observed in all good managers. On one occasion MEL was in danger of losing its computer to the central computer group in Philips. IBM indoctrinated them into centralising all computer activities on one mainframe computer. The Computer Manager at

MEL, John Duncan, prepared a long and detailed report listing a host of reasons why not. The Managing Director, Richard Rankin, in a brief meeting, casually flicked through the report, asked a few questions and to John's distress put it in his out tray with hardly a comment.

Actually Rankin had spotted the one key argument needed for MEL to keep its computer. At the key decision meeting the triumphant Dutch Executive pressing for centralisation was flabbergasted when Rankin simply said MEL couldn't give up its computer because MEL operated in the Defence Sector and was covered by the Official Secrets Act' He therefore was unable to discuss the matter further! I still chuckle when I think about it.

Whatever happened to that unwise promise of the 'paperless office? All managers are nowadays bombarded by masses and masses of information. It is not unusual for papers for a monthly board meeting to run to 50 or more pages. This is despite the ability of computer applications to drill down and process data in real time and every which way. The central reality is that managers need relevant information in the right format to suit the occasion and not indiscriminate data. Only a manager can decide what is relevant to him or her in a particular situation and what is relevant continually changes and mutates dynamically in a way it is impossible to predict or track. The dreams of the Management Information Systems experts are just that - dreams.

Unfortunately, in the modern world we seem to increasingly worship at the altar of complexity and lose touch with reality and relevance. This book is littered, I regret to say, with words like complex[xvii] and complicated. The truth, of course, is that simple things work well and complex ones work badly (if at all) because they are not robust. As even Scottie in Star Trek once remarked: "The more complicated the plumbing, the easier it is to block the drains".

Some books on management stress the need for what they call strategic thinking or strategic intent, whatever they are supposed to be. I have yet to see a clear and succinct definition of strategy or strategic thinking although I have read loads of waffle on the subject. For the little it is worth, I define strategy as 'a jigsaw of the obvious'. Strategy is ultimately only about what needs to be done and when and usually because the obvious is often anything but obvious!

There is a lot of pseudo-intellectual snobbery and hocus-pocus about strategic thinking. The word strategic evokes a reverential and hushed response as if thinking in strategic terms means ascending into the intellectual stratosphere.

Lee Scott, the chief executive of the highly successful Wal-Mart said "our-long term strategy is to be where we are not.' I somehow doubt if business school theorists would regard this as strategic thinking but actually it is one of the finest examples of strategic thinking I have encountered. I once worked to help the Board of a company devise a

---

[xvii] Stafford Beer in *Brain of the Firm* suggests that a company of only 300 there are 3×10^{92} bits of information!

strategy. After a number of long and painful sessions they agreed it was 'To be the best.' To the outsider this may seem a platitude. To those inside the company it encapsulated their values and the pride they had in their products, staff and traditions.

Andy Kilpatrick, the outstanding headmaster referred to in chapter 9, illustrates his approach to strategy by contrasting the two ways of taking the high ground. One is to prepare a detailed plan for overcoming opposition step by step and then press on rigidly and regardless of cost or obstacles. This is the classic military strategy of attrition: the set piece battle of the First World War. Unfortunately cads like Napoleon do not always play by set piece rules. Their much better strategy is to take the top of the hill first and mop up the enemy afterwards.

Andy would I believe agree that good strategies are characterised by Vision, Wisdom, Credibility, Simplicity, Audacity, Focus and Action.

ELEMENTS IN STRATEGIC THINKING

VISION "When there is no vision the people perish". Vision is an integral part of strategy and should reflect the values, hopes and aspirations of the organisation.
WISDOM Successful strategies are always based on wisdom, knowledge and experience.
CREDIBLE For a strategy to be more than mere words it has to be credible, practical and realistic.
SIMPLE A strategy must always be simple and clear because ordinary mortals have to implement it. Complex strategies never work.
AUDACIOUS Audacity and courage are the steel of strategy. It is hard to think of a successful strategy, which was not audacious.
FOCUSSED The success of a strategy stems from a narrow front approach and a single-minded focus on what needs to be done.
ACTION Visions are idles dreams unless they are given work to do. The essence of a strategy is action and vitality for transforming ideas into reality.

A strategy is clearly a synthesis and managers who think in strategic terms do so in multi-dimensional terms. They have a picture in their minds, which relates all the aspects and facets to each other in a coherent way. This does not mean thinking in complex terms. The essence of effective thinking in management is to keep thoughts 'one mind' size. A cardinal precept of 'thinking to do' is that at any level, bottom to top, all tasks or policies are 'one mind' size. One mind size does not mean one level. It means a picture in the mind of *all* the *relevant* details. Anything which is more than 'one mind' sized is unworkable because who is the genius out there who can share minds?

Some managers suppose they simply need the high level picture ('don't bother me with the details'). That is rarely true. Managers need the high level picture and often the *relevant* low-level detail. This is emphatically not *all* the detail. The manager whose mind is cluttered with too much information cannot think clearly. Human minds are like umbrellas: they work best when they are open and hardly work at all when they are closed.

All the world's greatest strategists and leaders have always enunciated wisdom with elegant and eloquent simplicity and incisive clarity. Sun Tzu: 'Those who are certain to capture what is attacked, attack locations which are not defended'. Napoleon: 'Unhappy the general who comes on the field of battle with a system.' Saki: 'In baiting a mouse trap with cheese, always leave room for the mouse'. Achieving elegant simplicity and incisive clarity requires clear thinking and is very, very difficult but it makes a huge difference.

A lot of management thinking is about confused and confusing issues – the fog of management. Something seems not quite right but a manager does not understand why. The indications are unclear. This is why instinctive knowing and self-knowledge is an important part of a manager's thinking process. The things, which we all know deep down, are often difficult if not impossible to articulate. As a consequence, they are not amenable to rational analysis. No manager should dismiss what he or she knows, but all managers should have some kind of audit mechanism within themselves to ensure their knowing is not a fantasy. All managers need internal checks and balances as well as external ones.

I think of my personal audit mechanism almost in biblical terms. It is akin to walking through the valley of the shadow of death. Whenever I had to take a difficult or complex decision as a manager I always went through a conscious and sub-conscious and lonely process of auditing and cross checking my reasons and motives.

Always I would argue with myself:

1. Why do I think this?
2. What are my personal motives?
3. Why am I wrong?
4. What is bad about it?
5. What is good?

This is a painful process. It is like looking inside yourself from outside. It is a form of 'opening your mind and asking 'is this the only way?' It means assuring yourself that on balance you have found a workable way while remembering others may have an even better workable way.

At the end of the day all managerial decisions come as much from conviction as they do from intellectual analysis and even the best and most successful decisions are as much subjective as they are objective. Nothing is wholly objective, even scientific research. Professor Gerald Holton examined the notebooks of Robert Millikan who won a Nobel Prize in 1923. The notebooks covered a period of one and a half years and Holton found that of 148 tests, only 58 coincided with Millikan's pre-suppositions. The other 90 tests gave different results so Millikan blithely ignored them because he "knew in his bones" they were wrong[xviii]!

Einstein had a similar approach. When Eddington sent Einstein the telegram 'We've confirmed your general theory of relativity, the sun's rays are bent' Einstein replied 'Well, I knew it would have to be so anyway.' One of his research students, Ilsa Rosenthal Schneider, expressed shock at Einstein's unscientific remark. She asked, "What would have happened if they have found the opposite?" Einstein replied "I would be very sorry for the dear Lord God, because the theory is right".[xix]

Decisions in management are never simplistic although they need to simple if they are to be effective. As Einstein

---

[xviii] *Script of broadcast interview of Professor Gerald Holton by Professor Lewis Wolpert 3rd August 1990 Source: BBC*
[xix] *ibid*

once remarked, "Nothing is so complicated that it cannot be simply explained. He also said things should be as simple as they need to be but never simpler. The distinction between simplistic and simple is especially important in management. Simple reaches the essence. Simplistic trivialises and is of no value.

In contrast, the notion that decision taking is about getting and analysing all the facts and information is nonsense. 'A decision is the action an executive must take when the information is so incomplete that the answer does not suggest itself.'[xx] Key decisions invariably involve dilemmas and paradox. There are no blacks or whites or simplistic choices.

Key decisions are rarely taken without organisational and sometimes personal risk. Some decisions are particularly painful and involve choosing the lesser evil. Managers in the real world sometimes have to face the need to decide on the basis of the greatest good for the greatest number. Such decisions are never pleasant, but they cannot be avoided. A manager can't walk away when the going gets tough as it always does at one time or another.

Sometimes the right decisions are made for the wrong reasons. I once authorised a significant investment to increase the output of a production unit in anticipation of receiving a large order from a customer. The order never came but we unexpectedly received our largest order ever from a source we had not expected. The order entailed increasing output in a year by 1200% and we achieved it

---

[xx] Arthur William Radford. *Time* Feb. 25th 1957.

with a marginal increase in staff because of the prior investment made for the wrong potential customer.

Numbers are often important in decision taking but may not be as important as many suppose. Decisions about large capital investments usually occupy a significant amount of managerial time. The consequences of mistakes are often small because in a successful organisation, there are always large cash flows from depreciation to provide a cushion. What is much more important is not the decision to invest but the *determination* to ensure the investment is successful.

That is why I concentrated on the credibility and track record of the people who prepared the proposal as well as the content. The proposal was most probably sound if the proposer could look me in the eye and answer three levels of 'why' questions, then. Asking "why" three times is incredibly powerful and revealing.

Successful management needs focus, necessity and action:

- A focus on what *needs* to be done,
- The necessity of *why* it needs to be done
- The action of *how* it will be done.

This cascading sequence of *what-why-how* is a simple and powerful way of thinking and making decisions because it directly maps on to reality.

When we think we theorise but that is not the same as picking a theory from a book and trying to make it work. Theories should help us when we think and be part of the synthesis the mind produces. No sensible manager re-invents the wheel. But when we rely on off the shelf theories of others we are in effect using second hand thinking instead of using our own brains. As likely as not this means trying to shoehorn our reality into an irrelevant theory. Our politically correct culture seems to place a premium on asking experts and pseudo-experts instead of standing on our own feet and relying on our staff and ourselves. This is political and managerial correctness gone stark, staring, raving mad once again.

'Thinking to do' is ultimately about choosing and deciding and managers have to do that themselves. No one can do it for them. Managerial leadership, if it is about anything, is about the action of translating thoughts in the mind into reality in the world. That is best achieved by doers who think, or by thinkers who do but not by thinkers who theorise. The problem is that far, far too many managers are thinkers who theories and far too many thinkers who do instead of doers who think. It is a profound and debilitating mistake.

Fantasy or Reality?

Chapter 11 - Make Things Happen

The world can only be grasped by action, not by contemplation... The hand is the cutting edge of the mind
- JACOB BRONOWSKI The Ascent of Man (1973)

Management should be about action. It is about making things happen and getting things done. The common sense element of doing so is to 'keep it simple stupid (KISS)' while not making the mistake of confusing simple with simplistic.

Leadership is also integral to management. No one can make things happen if they cannot lead, motivate as well as organise. A computer can be managed, people need to be led. An organisation without leadership is like a headless chicken. It is why this book uses the term 'managerial leadership' as success requires a good leader with vision and wide experience as well as good organisational skills.

Getting things done is not about complicated theories, grand designs or rushing in where even fools fear to tread. Such approaches fail, often disastrously so. To make things happen a managerial leader needs to think, plan and prepare *before* taking action not afterwards. Abraham Lincoln said. "If I had 6 hours to cut down a tree, I would spend 4 hours sharpening the axe". Really wise managerial leaders do exactly that – but it is not easy.

Clarity in what needs to be done and why is essential, as is the need to divorce these from the how. Too many managerial leaders fail because they confuse the two.

Successful leaders think through what needs to be done and why. They then delegate the task of working out the details of 'how' to their subordinates. Managers who meddle or wallow in detail sow the seeds of failure and never get the best out of their staff. A stonemason does not have to be told how to chisel the stone but may need to be told the order in which stones need to be chiselled.

Delegation of the "how" does not mean abdication or no detail. Often a managerial leader needs to know and understand the crucial detail but not *all* the details. A good manager has a light touch plus an instinct for understanding what is relevant and when he or she needs to intervene or leave well alone.

The buck should nevertheless always stop with the manager who should never be able to plead ignorance as far too many now do. To make it absolutely clear, management is about both setting a task and monitoring progress in implementing the task as outlined in the table overleaf.

Making things happen is however not quite as simple and logical as the table overleaf may suggest. Things very rarely work out in such a simple, logical fashion and some of the actions are much more difficult than they may seem to be. It is not an easy thing to ensure actions are clear, simple and practical.

I have spent hours, even days as a consultant, helping hard-pressed managers to figure out what they really want and to then express it in a way others clearly understand.

THE COMMON SENSE OF MAKING THINGS HAPPEN

1. Check each action to ensure it is CLEAR, SIMPLE AND PRACTICAL. Ask someone not directly involved if they understand each action. If they don't re-draft and re-draft until they do.
2. Ensure there is an owner and a precise timetable for each action.
3. Check for understanding and for emotional and intellectual acceptance. Remember people who believe achieve.
4. Limit the number of action items to a maximum of 5 for any one person. Three would be better.
5. Select actions by balancing two criteria:
   - IMPORTANCE
   - SPEED

(Quick successes are wonderful for starting the ball rolling, hence the use of speed.)

6. Avoid actions that are never ending. You must be able to clearly monitor progress and not get bogged down in detail.
7. Turn soft statements into clear time-defined outcomes and/or hard numbers. Vagueness is out, OK?
8. Check each action to ensure there are:
   - No jargon statements
   - No acronyms
   - No motherhood statements
   - No generalities
   - No slogans
   - No theories
   - No models
9. Be bold and turn can't into can.
10. Look for achievement, not excuses.
11. Get on with it *now* – not to-morrow.

Reading a theory in a book is not the same as doing something and making it happen. The latter often needs a lot of precious time, patience and care – commodities usually in short supply in the pressurised managerial environment.

The maxim "What gets measured gets done" is a good one except that if everything gets measured, bureaucracy, inefficiency and all-mighty confusion results and nothing gets done.

One remarkable leader in the public sector, who made things happen and avoided this trap, was Admiral Sir John Fisher - First Sea Lord from 1904-10 and 1914-15. He cut British naval estimates year after year while steadily increasing the fighting power of the British Navy. Luxury expenditure was slashed: the maintenance of half a dozen frigates for social purposes in every port from Mombasa to Hong Kong was stopped. The building of dreadnoughts, battleships with much greater speed and firepower, went to the top of the expenditure list[i]. If only public sectors in the UK had leaders with such calibre, drive and vision today. What a difference it would make to say the NHS, Education, Police or Defence.

The growth of inefficiency in the navy since Fisher's time was starkly illustrated by figures (overleaf) compiled by Northcote Parkinson:[ii] The navy circa 2015 has more Admirals than ships; a massive aircraft carrier that will be in service for some years without aircraft; and a second

[i] Antony Jay Management and Machiavelli

[ii] C Northcote Parkinson Parkinson's Law (London: Penguin Books reprint 2002) ISBN 0-141-18685-2.p20. It is a timeless repository of wisdom and common sense. It is astonishing how many have read it yet how much it is ignored.

carrier that if completed and not sold, will only have helicopters. Look at the figures below, what a shambles!

Classification	1914	1928	% increase or decrease
Capital ships in commission	62	20	-67.74
Officers and men in Royal Navy	146,000	100,000	-31.5
Dockyard workers	57,000	62,439	+9.54
Dockyard officials and clerks	3,249	4,558	+40.28
Admiralty officials	*2,000*	*3,569*	*+78.45*

A manager is a manager is a manager. The central task of managerial leadership in any organisation is to decide what needs to be done and ensure it is done outstandingly well. Managing a school, conducting an orchestra, leading a company, running a hospital, captaining a ship are all similar in managerial terms. They are all dealing with people and maximising the ratio of output to input in order to make the required beneficial difference. The disciplines and constraints of a profit motive undoubtedly sharpen and provide a focus for making things happen. Managers in the private sector *have* to be entrepreneurial. With all the recent austerity measures and cost constraints in the Public Sector, there is, thank goodness, a growing recognition of the need for enterprise and efficiency too.

The criticisms frequently raised that the public sector cannot be managed like the private sector misses the point that management is always much more effective when it is fully accountable for its performance. Management, which is not accountable, is, to borrow a phrase a British Prime Minister, Stanley Baldwin, once used about the press 'the prerogative of the harlot throughout the ages'. There are regrettably, still many harlots in and around both private and particularly public sector management to this day.

The big advantage of the profit motive in making things happen is that the success or otherwise of doing so is reduced to one number. That number, the net profit, is the small difference between two large figures and it is the result of a multiplicity of actions and activities. The public sector does not enjoy such simplicity and has instead to substitute achieving for performance targets for net profit. If these do not reflect reality – and they often don't – all kinds of problems arise.

Another consequence is that inefficiency is institutionalised because market forces never put a failing public sector activity out of business. To private sector management it seems amazing how virtually anything new a government does always seems to need more resources. In the UK the parrot-cry is always "new money" yet it is remarkable how little productivity seems to improve if at all. My perception is that it often goes downhill.

The really important lesson is that nothing gets done just by chance or by leaving well alone. The one thing organisational systems have in common with physical systems is that, left to themselves, they will decay and become disordered. It is called entropy or sometimes 'Murphy's Law' that states if anything can go wrong it will do so. For beneficial things to happen there has to be a conscious process or plan of action to get things done and the energy and enthusiasm to do so. To make things happen there has to be focus, plan, purpose, action, organisation and continuity. It is what managerial leadership is or should be about as is empowering subordinates rather than being prescriptive or enmeshed in 'the how'.

Peter Drucker once said 'the purpose of an organisation was to make common men do uncommon things, but the purpose of managerial leadership was to make common men into uncommon men'.[iii] I wholeheartedly concur with this view. To paraphrase Bronowski, quoted at the frontispiece of this chapter, getting things done can only be achieved by action.

[iii] *Ibid Peter Drucker page 137*

Fantasy or Reality?

Chapter 12 - Respect Human Nature

It is only when you work with rather than against people that achievement and lasting success is possible- Sir JOHN HARVEY-JONES

and/but ...

Human action can be modified to some extent, but human nature cannot be changed - ABRAHAM LINCOLN

To get the best out of an organisation a leader has to get the best out of the people in it. Outstanding leaders have always instinctively understood this simple and common sense truth. They clearly understand that to motivate people they have to be treated as human beings and not as machines or wage slaves.

Too often managers, like politicians, don't do this and work against the grain of human nature. They bring the worst out of people rather than the best. In order to get the best out of people managerial leaders need to be cognisant about human nature and the nature of work. Human beings are both simple and complicated. They are simple in that they all have basic needs. They are complicated in their individual ambitions, beliefs, dreams and prejudices. At one level people want and need to belong. At another level they want to preserve their individuality and privacy. This is why leadership is as much, or more, about being instinctive than it is intellectual and why it is hard work. It is about hearts and minds.

There are two sayings used in the north of England about people. One is 'there is nowt (nothing) so queer as folks'. The other is 'Everyone is queer except thee and me and I am not sure about thee'! In the loftier language of an

189

Fantasy or Reality?

American intellectual, Richard Hofstadter: 'Human beings are tissues of contradictions and the life even of the intellectual is not logic but experience.'[i]

The reality is that we are all a complex mixture. We all do what we think is right. Thieves don't believe stealing is wrong even though they face punishment if caught. Al Capone regarded himself as a public benefactor. One Warden of Sing-Sing prison in said in his experience 'few of the criminals in Sing-Sing regard themselves as bad men.'[ii]

None of us are angels. We are all self-seeking and not entirely rational about it contrary to what Economists assume. We all take foolish personal decisions and do foolish things. Individuals or groups who believe their best interests are threatened will go to inordinate lengths and use considerable ingenuity to protect their interests. So managers with any sense will only impose adverse changes on people when they have literally no alternative as happens in crisis situations. Doing so carries a heavy price in human, motivational and therefore managerial terms.

Although there may be no immutable, universal truths we all nevertheless have personal immutable and unchangeable truths built into our psyches and these influence what we believe, feel and think and how we

---

[i] *Richard Hofstadter Anti-Intellectualism in American Life (New York – Vintage Books 1963) ISBN 0-394-70317-0 p 32*
[ii] *Dale Carnegie How to Win Friends and Influence People (England – World's Work Ltd 1983) p 32*

behave. Some personal immutable truths may be socially undesirable and deep seated like racialism but it is pointless to deny they exist or to believe they can easily be changed.

According to Abraham Lincoln 'Human action can be modified to some extent, but human nature cannot be changed'. Managers can force people to behave in certain ways; they can regulate what their staff does and how they do it, they can bully and coerce, they can influence hearts and minds. What they cannot change or influence are people's immutable truths or tell them what and how to think or believe. Leaders have to get the best out of people as they are, warts and all, and not how they ideally want them to be.

Work is always a social as well as an economic activity but not all work for all people is interesting and stimulating. Some work is boring and tedious and some is distinctly unpleasant. Just as in the home, someone has to do domestic chores, such as washing up, so in organisations there are always essential but unpleasant tasks to be performed. Work, like life, never was, never is and never will be a bed of roses. Come to think of it, who would want to sleep on a bed of roses anyway?

For many work is *primarily* an economic chore although, despite what the mechanistic and the so-called scientific school of management and Marxists say or believe, it is rarely if ever *purely* economic. We all get some social and other satisfaction from our work even those who perform the most humdrum of tasks. Pride in work is not confined

191

to those with the most stimulating and lucrative jobs, managerial or otherwise. We have all met poorly paid cleaners and others who rightly have immense pride in what they do and the high standards they achieve. When people feel what they do is important they do it well.

Pride is important in motivation: pride in the organisation, pride in the personal contribution towards it, pride in achievement, pride in its products or services and pride in its ethos and reputation. These are the real catalysts for motivation. Money is, of course, a motivator but is no substitute for personal pride and self-respect and is never ever by itself effective. Indeed it is often a corrosive influence as is evident from the near criminal activities of parts of the banking and financial sector.

Three stonemasons were once asked what they did. One said: "I earn a living, guv." Another said: "I chisel stone". The third proudly said: "I build cathedrals"[iii]. The more people in an organisation who believe they are building cathedrals the more successful it will be. It is unrealistic to suppose it is possible to persuade everyone to believe they are building cathedrals although there are periods when it happens and that really is magic. It is the ideal all leaders should always aim for.

Belief is clearly important in getting the best out of people particularly if they believe they are building cathedrals. Unfortunately belief is a two-edged sword and can and is

---

[iii] Dr Sheila Sheinberg Managing Transformation published in The Journal of Quality Management March 1991. JQM is published by Marian College, 45 South National Avenue, Fond Du Lac WI 54935, USA.

used to bring the worst out of people. Throughout the ages bullies, dictators and tyrants have always too clearly understood how important beliefs are (see chapter 2). They have found it only too easy to cynically foster beliefs based on prejudices and fears and to construct/impose mass belief systems and bring out the worst in human nature. There are inevitably some managers who are petty tyrants and who work this way.

We used to classify workers as manual and non-manual and this has influenced perceptions about the nature of work. It is arguable, however, that all work is brainwork in one form or another. Brawn can never be used without the brain and it is interesting that some 50% of the cells in the cerebral cortex are devoted to the control of our hands so in one sense we almost think with our hands. Manual workers use their brains via their hands. The skills of a craftsman are impressive. Non-manual workers use their brains via their mouths and their hands to write, type and communicate. The classification of manual and non-manual really is artificial, misleading and above all divisive.

All human beings have limitations but the biggest mistake most managers make is to underestimate what people can do rather than overestimate them. People are often much brighter and more creative than we think. When I left university in 1961, Bryan Glastonbury[iv],John Mills[v], Louis

---

[iv] *Before he retired was Professor Glastonbury at Southampton University.*

[v] *Author of a number of books on economic policy including Tackling Britain's False Economy, Europe's Economic Dilemma, Managing the World Economy and Exchange Rate Alignments. Founder and chairman of JML.*

Nhentenda[vi] and myself did an investment study in Nyasaland (now Malawi). As part of the study we spent some time in Southern Rhodesia (now Zimbabwe) visiting various industries. In that white dominated country we were given innumerable reasons why native Africans could not do skilled jobs. In Nyasaland we found Africans doing the jobs we had been categorically assured they could not do.

The truth is that human beings with belief, self-confidence and motivation can almost perform miracles. Getting the best out of human nature is about fostering these. It never ceases to amaze me how able and creative people are given the right environment.

There is rightly a great deal of emphasis nowadays on team building and there is no doubt people working as a team can perform miracles as I have seen again and again in my career. There is no better more effective way of getting the best out of human nature.

Teams work best when they have a clear focus and objectives. They need an 'outer' leader to set the agenda of *what* has to be done and explain *why,* someone not intimately involved on a day-to-day basis. For that they need a team leader, an 'inner' leader who is an integral part of the group and concentrates on the *how.* The outer leader is akin to an admiral who directs the overall course of a sea battle. The inner leader is akin to a captain who carries out the Admiral's orders. The team leader needs a

---

[vi] *An undergraduate from Nyasaland at Salisbury University.*

narrow focus, the leader outside the team has a wider focus.

A word of caution before any one charges off with the idea this is a new theory of leadership. The description of inner and outer leaders is an abstraction used to describe different aspects of leadership:

1. The *what* and *the why.*
2. The *how* of doing so.

In some cases one person performs both leadership roles. For example a commander of a small group of fighting ships may also perform the role of captain of his own ship. And leadership is never static. Someone who does not have the rank of leader in the official organisation, but is the silver fox esteemed by his or her peers, may sometimes (or often!) exercise de facto leadership.

Teams can, of course, contribute in suggesting *what* should be done but ultimately the decision has to be that of the leader. President Kennedy was the outer leader, the ultimate decision maker, who took the decision to put a man on the moon. Without his decision and support nothing would have happened but it would not have happened either without a team of dedicated individuals at NASA and other supporting institutions.

The most important aspect in team building is that the team should collectively decide *how*. This incidentally is why small groups in the SAS work so well and why they are so effective. Teams do *not* provide leadership but they respond magnificently to inspired leadership, which gives them freedom to think and act. The idea of 'leaderless teams' is an oxymoron. One of the biggest disservices the Management Myth Making Industry has done to management is to foster the belief that committees make sensible decisions. They don't and they can't. 'A committee's purpose is to help a man decide'[vii].

The idea that committees in organisations are democratic decision bodies is as wrong-headed as the idea that each person should have an equal voice and vote. That never was so and never will be. The value of an individual's contribution to a group or committee should depend on their ability, expertise, judgement, manipulative and persuasive skills, their standing and wisdom. We are not all equal in ability and never will be but we are all surely entitled to respect and honest treatment. The concept of a decision-making committee is an ideology imported from the political arena where it is does not work. Even in a democracy, some are considerably more equal than others. It is no accident that the Prime Minister is 'primus inter pares' (first among equals).

The most frequent method of criticising a committee is to say that a camel is a horse designed by a committee. That is misplaced since camels have remarkable powers of endurance, much greater than horses, and there is no way a committee could possibly design something as good as a camel.

When teams decide *what* to do instead of concentrating on *how* they usually make an almighty cock-up of it. Microsoft

---

[vii] Antony Jay *Corporation Man* (London: The Professional Library 1972) p 91

has, in my subjective opinion, inflicted some awful software on the planet usually because a large, bureaucratic committee conceived it. There were too many deciding and too few doing as is always the case in large bureaucracies.

It is interesting that the highly successful VMS operating system, used on the VAX computers that propelled Digital to success, was conceived by a group of less than ten people. Microsoft's NT system, based partly on VMS, had a huge team working on it.[viii]

With expectations of work increasing all the time, especially as living and educational standards improve, we too easily forget that work provides for deep-seated human needs: recognition and rituals, rhythms and routines, goals and incentives, shared objectives and values and discipline and rules. The key role of the leader is to create an organisational environment where human needs are met but without compromising what needs to be done.

Human beings crave recognition. We all want to feel important, liked and loved. That is why management by talking to and listening to people and where possible praising their achievements is so important in getting the best out of people. With our obsession with technology and with the increasing emphasis on financial incentives we are in danger of forgetting the simple truth that people

---

[viii] *Fredrick P Books Jr explains in the Mythical Man-month (London: Addison-Wesley 1982) IBBN 0-201-00650-2 why throwing resources at software development often makes matters worse rather than better.*

take pride in their work and love to talk about what they do.

As a manager I used to spend a significant part of my time walking about and talking to the people who worked for me and that included evening factory visits to talk to shift workers. Far too many managers nowadays are so meeting-bound that they never ask them or almost even know they exist. This is particularly true in the large, monolithic bureaucracies in both public and private sectors. Simply treat people as numbers or as machines and they will behave and work accordingly.

Most outstanding leaders understand how effective leadership by walking around is. One reason is symbolic: the effect it has on people. Another is that leaders who spend time walking around learn what the real problems are. Winston Churchill, for instance, found from a visit to one airfield that 7 out of 10 qualified pilots were in desk jobs at a time when there was a chronic shortage of pilots – a situation Churchill very quickly caused to be changed.

Management by walking about, trusting, asking and listening to people is equally effective with customers. Sir Terry Leahy, at the time, CEO of the UK retailer Tesco said that 'asking customers what improvements they would like to their local store and then delivering them costs *half as much* as letting top designers of the retail world dictate'[ix].

[ix] Quoted in <u>The Times</u> 15th January 2003

Roger Holmes when he joined Marks and Spencer as Head of Retail, spent most of his first 12 months with the company visiting the stores and talking to customers and staff. He recruited six customers who he took round the stores at intervals to gauge their reactions to the improvements the company were trying to make.[x]

Good managers have empathy for people. 'Jefferson put it that men by their constitution were naturally divided into two parts: those who fear and distrust the people versus those who identify with the people have confidence in them. Our civilisation has increasingly put those who fear and distrust in power over us.'[xi]

One of the few exceptionally good academic studies of management is the well-known Hawthorne Experiment conducted in the 1920's by Elton Mayo[xii]. He and his colleagues found that the productivity of a group of workers, who originally produced 2,400 relays a week, improved irrespective of whether conditions were made better or made worse:

- Piecework was introduced - Output went up.
- Five-minute rest pauses introduced - Output went up.
- Rest pauses doubled - Output went up.

---

[x] *Judi Bevan The Rise & Fall of Marks & Spencer (London: Profile Books 2002) p 247*
[xi] *John Ralston Saul Voltaire's Bastards - The Dictatorship of Reason in the West (New York: Vintage Books 1993) ISBN 0-679-74819-9 p584*
[xii] *J A C Brown The Social Psychology of Industry (London – Pelican Books 1961) p 71-2*

- Work ended at 4.30 pm instead of 5 pm - Output went up
- Work ended at 4 pm - Output went up.

Finally all the improvements were taken away: work on Saturday, forty-eight hour week, no rest pauses, no piecework and no free meal. Output at 3,000 relays per week was the highest ever.

They concluded that the only explanation was the group studied increased productivity because of the attention focussed on them. The workers felt wanted and important. Many managers have heard of the Hawthorne Studies yet ignore the findings and fail to draw the obvious conclusions from them, namely that people work better when they are motivated and receive recognition and, yes, love.

One way of giving recognition is to inflate job titles, an American practice finding increasing favour in Europe more's the pity. In the United States the title Office Manager has now become virtually defunct and has been replaced by titles such as Stock Control and Incident Manager or Regional Head of Services or Senior Vice-President of Global Procurement. A window cleaner now incredibly has the title Optical Illuminator Enhancer. A lavatory cleaner has become a Technical Sanitation Assistant. Titles advertised in the UK include "Real Nappy Project Development Officer", "Air Action Officer" and "Occupational Kinesiology Therapist" and the numbers are growing daily.

Personally, while recognising that all human beings deserve esteem and respect for the work they do, I hate the idea of the deception and self-deception involved in distorting job titles. This is because it devalues people and is managerial double-speak taken to extremes. It smacks of political correctness of the worst kind. Yet nearly half of the 1,700 people, who responded to a workplace survey in the UK conducted by reed.co.uk said 'uptitling' (a horrible American word) would make them happier at work. It takes all sorts to make a world!

Rituals are as, or more, important than fancy job titles in getting the best out of people. They may be falling out of favour because they can be perceived as paternalistic and politically incorrect. But the use of rituals to recognise service or achievement meets a deep human need. They can take many forms, from a Friday beer bash to formal awards, ceremonies and certificates.

Mintzberg[xiii] in his studies of the work managers *actually* do, as distinct from what the theories suggest they *should* do, found that performing ritual and ceremonial duties such as giving out gold watches, presiding at Christmas dinners, attending company social functions were an intrinsic part of a chief executive's job. There is a great danger in modern society of under estimating the importance of rituals and symbolism in helping to provide social cohesion in an organisation. We tend to mistakenly

---

[xiii] *Henry Mintzberg The Nature of Managerial Work (New York: Harper & Row) 1973 ISBN 0-06-044556-4 and Henry Mintzberg* <u>Folklore and Fact</u> - *Harvard Business Review July/August 1975*

see organisations and the people in them in a narrow, mechanistic sense.

With seven-day services, 24 hours a day, we are also in danger of forgetting the importance of rhythms and routines and how they fulfil deep-seated and instinctive human needs. Schools and universities have seasons, rhythms and routines around which all their activities revolve and it is noticeable how well managed and run many are. They are geared to receiving students at one age, ideally promoting a love of learning and then passing them elsewhere for the next stage in their lives. This cycle is underpinned by yearly, term, weekly and daily cycles and routines. They all fit together and provide a sense of continuity, permanence, stability and a feeling of belonging. From the outside, the academic-life seems to have an attractive and almost feudal nature; a kind of oasis of tranquillity. I am sure it feels anything but from the inside!

Creating this kind of ambiance in other organisations would do wonders for getting the best out of people, but it is often not possible because of the dynamic and changing environments in which many organisations work. There is a university of life but life is not a university.

At one stage in my career I learnt the hard way how deeply engrained cycles and rhythms are. There were five batch-production divisions under me and at the end of each calendar month there was frantic pressure in each of them to meet their production outputs. This caused bottlenecks in the packing and other departments who provided a common service for the divisions.

No matter what I said or did, the end of calendar month rush stubbornly persisted. So I naively invented a four-week cycle to smooth the workflow and gave each divisional manager a different end week. It didn't work. There was still the same almighty rush, panic and pressure at the end of each calendar month to get the products out. In the majority of organisations there is always an end of month and often, end of financial year pressures to make sales, meet production targets and collect debts. There are few organisations where the workload is constant day-by-day, week-by-week or month-by-month.

Seasons and cycles are part of our make-up and human beings sub-consciously adjust to them. This is often reflected in order patterns. In one department I managed we always used to get an influx of orders just before the summer holiday period started. It seemed the last task of our customers before they went on summer holiday was to get their orders out so that when they returned from holidays they could get cracking on their production before the Christmas breaks. Similar kinds of people and organisational induced peaks happen in many organisations at Christmas. They then gear down for Christmas and start with a flourish in the New Year.

Some cycles and rhythms are self-induced. One company I saw had a Managing Director who loved special offers and promotions: 2 for 1, 40% off etc. When we examined the promotions we found that all they did was to create artificial peaks and troughs. When there was a promotion demand soared upwards and soared downwards immediately afterwards. This increased the overhead since it tended to be geared to the self-created peaks and inflated non-peak stocks. There was no evidence they led to a permanent increase in market share but the MD felt good about them. He had obviously read too many marketing books!

From time to time, communication becomes the fashionable cure-all for motivation in the Management Myth Making Industry and is a perennial topic. All the ills of an organisation are at times ascribed to poor communication and small fortunes are spent on jazzing up internal communications through setting up briefing groups, producing videos and the like. The vast majority of such initiatives are a cosmetic seven-day wonder. They are set up with a fanfare of trumpets only to quickly fall by the wayside, as everybody except management, knew they would.

That said, the communications gurus do have a point. Babel was man's second major engineering undertaking after Noah's Ark and the first major communication fiasco. It had a clear, if naive, mission but that was not the cause of failure. It had plenty of manpower, materials were in abundant supply in Mesopotamia and there were no time constraints. The pyramidal structure was inherently stable and spread the compressive load well so there were no problems with the technology. The undertaking failed because it lacked communication - the result of poor organisation and leadership or an act of God depending on your viewpoint.[xiv]

The central and obvious truth, which the communications Gurus miss or ignore, is that actions count much more than words. What management *does* has a much greater influence on people in an organisation than what they *say*. Leadership by example does not have a good press in modern management theories. The theorists are too obsessed with higher theoretical concerns such as core competencies, strategic intent, knowledge management or whatever happens to be in fashion. Too often a poor management says one thing and does the opposite They behave in one way but expect their staff to behave in another. Then they wonder why morale and performance is poor and bring in consultants to advise them.

One of the many paradoxes about people is how tolerant and forgiving they are and how well they will work even in poor conditions if they are motivated as the Hawthorne study showed. This is particularly evident in wartime and crisis situations. In the Second World War the allied forces tried to bomb the Germans into submission but when Cologne was literally reduce to rubble by bombs, the working civilian population actually increased their output.

There need to be rules and regulations, formal and informal, in all organisations. People work best when there is organisation and order. They need cohesion and need to know what is expected of them and what the limits are.

With the modern emphasis on individual rights there needs to be, more than ever before, a corresponding emphasis on responsibilities. When rights are divorced from responsibilities there is chaos. Within organisations it is the job of management to provide order and prevent disorder.

Informal rules are frequently more important than formal ones. The informal ones are part of the organisation culture and reflect its aspirations, taboos and values. "This is how we do things here". They are rarely, if ever, written down but everyone in the organisation knows what they are.

From the perspective of the managed, the ideal manager is open, fair, even-handed and consistent[xv]. The problem is that managers cannot always be consistent. When circumstances quickly change, as they do, even normally conciliatory managers have at times to ride rough shod over people and their feelings.

Many individuals would prefer not to have targets of any kind (we all like an easy life) but targets are important and necessary in all organisations. People need targets: they stretch, they enthuse, they motivate and they provide milestones and purpose. Badly conceived, they de-motivate in no time at all. Setting and imposing a multiplicity of conflicting, unrealistic and ill-considered ever changing targets is a certain way of promoting dishonesty, corrupting the integrity of an organisation and

---

[xv] *But individuals never seem to mind if a manager is little fairer to them than others. It is called privilege!*

bringing the worst out of human nature. Such target setting causes organisational cancer and chaos.

Individuals can at most handle seven variables (and that is probably 4 too many) but in bureaucracies they are often beset with a multiplicity of stupid targets. In theory a balanced scorecard is a means of improvement through balanced targets. In practice, they more often than not contain a multiplicity of both vague and subjective targets which, can be neither met nor measured. The balanced score card is, of course, largely a gimmick like so much else promoted by the Management Myth Making Industry.

Successful leaders and their organisations make the maximum use of intelligence and human ingenuity. Too many make minimum use, discourage initiative and then puzzle over their failures. Good managers treat people as adults, not wayward children (even though sometimes groups behave like adolescents) and recognise people need to learn by making mistakes. They respect and value their staff as human beings and treat and trust them accordingly. That is what really counts in motivating staff to work as though they believe they really are building cathedrals.

Fantasy or Reality?

Chapter 13 - Change the Organisation

It is best not to change something if changing it will not do any good
- TSUREZUREGUSA of KENKA - Essays in Idleness

Changing an organisation for the better is difficult. It is one of the most daunting but unavoidable tasks managers sometimes face. Yet all and sundry in the Management Myth Making Industry offer advice on how to manage change as if it was as simple as learning the two times table. Change to them is virtually a fad, a fashion mantra. There is certainly plenty of dubious information about managing change: a single search on the Internet in 2015 identified 369,000,000 entries!

In an ideal world change would be evolutionary, gradual and proactive. It is unfortunately reactive more often than not because pressures for change seem to erupt very quickly, rather like when a ship is caught in a gale. The essential factor then is calmness not panic. The problem is that managers with experience and skills in running a stable organisation may not have the skills or experience needed. They may not have the bottle to take the necessary painful decisions and act quickly and decisively when changes become inescapable. The change from a situation where everything seems to go right to a situation where everything suddenly seems to go wrong is a tough call to meet.

Actually the causal factors generating the need for reactive change are not always as bolt-out-of-the-blue as they may seem to be. They can and do result from a cumulative build-up of adverse factors that are recognised too late and result in a panicked response. This may be a consequence of not seeing the wood for the trees as discussed in Chapter 8. The writing may have been on the wall for a long time but to no avail. When everyone has their backs to that wall they don't notice it! It is essential therefore that the primary gaze of management is outward and customer centric and not inward and navel gazing.

Some changes happen because of a crisis when management has struggled but failed to rectify a worsening situation and has come to the end of its tether. When employees are then presented with a fait accompli feelings inevitably run very high particularly as it is the innocent who seem to always suffer and not the fat cats responsible. Witness the financial crisis of 2008 when some of those responsible received gold-plated pensions financed by taxpayer bailouts because of idiotic decisions made by the great and the good. I can still remember seeing Lord Mynors on TV waffling on trying to defend the indefensible.

Organisations cannot afford to stand still in a turbulent environment. They have to continually predict – through penetrative market research, client understanding and insight – and adapt to changes in their environment and markets. Not all managers have the prescience to recognise that the seeds of failure are often sown at the times of peak success. At such times there is an overriding feeling that nothing can go wrong and self-congratulation is the order of the day. Voices of doubt are not welcome.

There is always an underlying conflict between what an organisations ideally needs and what the people in them want. Organisations need to change. Employees on the other hand want continuity and stability. Changes, particularly far reaching ones, will therefore always produce tensions.

The change pundits claim the only constant is change and presented it as a profound truth when it is really a play on words. In reality, change may be confused with adaptation. It is the Darwinian survival of the adaptable that matters in organisational terms. Organisations cannot constantly face major disruptive changes and remain efficient.

Change is not a continuous revolutionary process as some may wrongly suppose. "If 3 billion years of evolution has made us what we are, do we really think that 100 days of revolution will change us?"[i] The tyrannical Chairman Mao thought so and caused human suffering on a gigantic scale. The danger is that change does more harm than good.

There is no shortage of change merchants offering advice - for a handsome fee. As Eileen Shjaprio, who was a McKinsley consultant, candidly admitted 'Change Management is the process of paying outsiders to create the pain that will motivate insiders to change, thereby transferring the change from the company's coffers into those of the consultants'. Quite so!

---

[i] R C Lewontin The Doctrine of DNA (Penguin Books – London 1993) ISBN 0-14-0232129-2 p90

The scope for managerial witch doctors is high. Some years ago, one peddled a one-day course 'Managing Organisation Change' for a bargain basement price. The blurb claimed delegates will learn about 'the effects of change on individuals and organisations'. They also packed into the event Change Management Models, Methods for Managing Change, plus the concept of 'Constant Change' and 'joined-up thinking'. Anyone who will believe that little lot will believe anything!

The reality is that it is impossible to learn how to do organisational change from a book, from a training course, by rote, nor by rigidly following a methodology or theory or by analytical techniques. Effective organisational change depends on humility, insight, intuition, judgement and leadership and you don't learn those from a book or at a seminar.

It is always wise to keep in mind that organisations are tribal entities with their own subtle cultures, pecking orders, traditions and values. Changing them disturbs the equilibrium, sometimes violently. There will always be winners and losers when an organisation changes. It is always a *political* process with a small "p" and requires a rare blend of leadership skills. It involves persuasion and pressure. It needs an ability to reconcile conflicting interests. It calls for a tolerance of uncertainty and ambiguity. It requires ruthless determination and drive to make change happen. Managing change is not for the faint hearted.

One of the fables used by the change merchants is that if you put a frog in a pot of water and warm it up slowly, the frog will placidly remain there until it is boiled to death. There are only two things wrong with the fable. First, it isn't true. According to Dr George R Zug, curator of reptiles and amphibians at the US National Museum of Natural history, 'Well that's, may I say, bullshit. If a frog had a means of getting out, it certainly would get out.'[ii] The second is that even if it were true, people are not frogs and don't behave like frogs.

Change is not the Eldorado it is made out to be in the voluminous literature on the subject. It is never as pure as the driven snow and the reasons for change are not always entirely objective, honest or sensible. Any fool can change (or ruin) an organisation. Regrettably too many fools are either in positions to do so, or to advise and influence those who are. Two heads may be better than one even if they are sheep's-heads but in management a lesser fool advising a superior fool is never a good thing!

In my experience there are five kinds of changes:

1. *Cosmetic change* - where change is a non-event.
2. *Change to* – where changes are imposed top down.
3. *Change with* - where those affected have some involvement in shaping change.
4. *Change by* - where changes are driven from the bottom of an organisation.

[ii] *www.fastcompany.com/online/01/frog.html*

5. *Change to and by* – where top down change metamorphoses to bottom up change.

Cosmetic change happens all too frequently, particularly in large organisations. They are often fashion or fad-based changes. For instance a Personnel Department changed to Human Relations, Quality Control upgraded to Quality Assurance, Knowledge Management replacing Information Management and so on. Such cosmetic changes are mostly self-serving. They of course feature 'appropriate' salary increases that may really be totally 'inappropriate'! Some are simply a game of management musical chairs. Others occur for purely presentational reasons.

Change to is an autocratic telling rather than a democratic asking. The pyramids would never have been built if the slaves had been politely asked to build them. There are *Change to* situations where management has to act first and explain afterwards. It is also true, however, that too many *Change to* situations are handled very unfairly and remarkably badly. One example that sticks in the gullet was when City Link in the UK was put into liquidation on Christmas Day 2014. That really was crass-stupidity and cruel to boot.

Most real changes are *Change to*. They arise for a variety of reasons including the loss of a major market or market share; the intrusion of economic reality; the inescapable need to drastically increase efficiency and cut costs bloated during the good times. Other factors causing *Change to* are the cumulative effects of company takeovers and major shifts in the market. These can include external Political,

Economic, Social and Technological influences that are difficult to near impossible to predict.

The greatest mistake with *Change to* is to make small cuts at the outset followed by a series of further cuts later. Nothing creates more demoralisation, fear and uncertainty amongst staff. It takes courage to make all the changes in one fell swoop but greatly aids the healing process afterwards. This is essential after major changes when an organisation has experienced major surgery.

Cisco had such courage when it hit a crisis. The Chief Executive John Chambers received a detailed daily report of orders received and noticed a mysterious drops in orders. He discovered from his counterparts in other companies that orders had dropped "like a light switch." Cisco had unfortunately built up a large stock to improve delivery times and was really exposed. The company went from a phenomenal growth rate of 70% a year to minus 30% within 45 days. It subsequently posted a massive loss of $2.9bn.

Chambers quickly and ruthlessly implemented *Change to* with a vengeance. Cisco made one really large staff cut and then started re-building the business and staff confidence. Morale was badly damaged but what was the alternative with such an external event driven change? Cisco survived. In 2014 its market capitalisation was about $129bn and it is one of the most valuable companies in the world.

This did not happen to Digital (Chapter 3) that made changes too little and too late. Had Digital possessed the foresight to even partly understand what was happening in its market place and made the changes that it finally made years later, much earlier, it may perhaps have survived.

Change with is more proactive than the reactive nature of *Change to*. In one company I advised, the Directors formulated a strategy for organisational change. They then had the courage and humility to invite a mixed group of employees to spend a day examining the strategy to feedback what they thought was wrong with it and why it would not work. The final combined strategy literally transformed the company and its fortune. In six months it had changed almost out of all recognition. The results were astonishing.

Change by, which is rarer, is even more astonishing. In one part of Digital in the UK, a new computer system was devised that enabled five administrative groups to be combined together to provide a much better service level. With the active involvement of the staff concerned the number was cut from 86 to 53, the managers reduced from 12 to 4 and 600 square metres of office space was cut. Salary costs were reduced by 40%.

All these changes were designed and implemented by the staff directly affected, with the help but not the direction, of internal consultants who were really 'emotion counsellors'. The direct involvement of the staff in the changes was highly emotional because they realised jobs would be lost. Some of the staff actually brought in teddy bears to cuddle when they were depressed.

The most remarkable change programme that I ever implemented was *Change to* that metamorphosed into *Change by* when I was Production Manager at MEL. At the time, MEL had to obtain certification for new Ministry of Defence quality standards, which seemed to me yet another bureaucratic imposition. Nevertheless, Bill Croft the Quality Assurance Manager succeeded in persuading me, against my better judgement, to attend a week's seminar with him.

By the fourth day I had become a convert for the new system. We skipped the last day and returned to make plans for rapidly improving quality assurance to prepare for the dreaded MOD inspection. We held a series of internal seminars based on what we had learned.

Much to the dismay of my management team I performed a volte-face and told them that they and all their staff had to attend two-day seminars on the subject. No discussion, no argument, attendance was compulsory. There are times in management where you have to ignore the maxim that you can take the horse to water but can't make it drink even if this means using a hosepipe to pour water down its throat!

The QA manager and I cleared our diaries to jointly run all the seminars to symbolically indicate their importance. The outcomes were electric. To start with participants were as sceptical as I had been but by the end of two days working through case studies they became emotionally and intellectually convinced. The word quickly spread on the grapevine and by the end of the last seminar the implementation developed its own momentum in the form of *Change by*. I doubt whether we could have stopped it. Everyone in the company was involved, bottom to top!

I have never been part of such a groundswell of change that was so quick, thorough and effective. Beforehand I had struggled to ensure the factory was tidy. Afterwards I could not have made it untidy! MEL passed its certification with flying colours. The MOD assessors were astonished at how knowledgeable the MEL staff were, especially when some helpfully pointed out things the assessors had missed!

Many changes are cost or crisis driven but the savings that result are often ephemeral and short lived. It is all too easy to cut costs in one place only to find they have increased somewhere else while no one was looking. When one company I know started to cut staff dramatically it was not uncommon to see staff leave on a Friday (with a handsome severance package) and return on Monday as temporary (i.e. semi-permanent) contractors on higher salaries. The head count fell but the costs actually increased and severance payments left a large hole in the balance sheet.

Most of us associate changes with widespread changes that involve a lot of staff but sometimes the enabling factor can be what may appear to be a minor or innocuous management decision such as the departure of an executive.

I once met the Chief Executive of a large group consisting of largely autonomous de-centralised and dissimilar companies who explained they only retained subsidiaries in their group if they could earn a large margin. If a subsidiary failed to do so they revisited the assumptions they had made about the company. If they decided their original assumptions had been wrong they sold it. If they thought they were right they replaced the managing director. The Chief Executive said that when a failed managing director was changed it was remarkable how the impossible suddenly became possible.

This very much reflects my own experience as a manager and consultant. On one occasion I had unfortunately to dismiss a manager of a factory that was, despite considerable help and support, a major headache. He was replaced with an existing member of my management team. The factory quickly ceased to be headache and became a major success.

As a consultant I have seen managing directors agonise for months about the performance of a key executive that somehow did not ring true before finally deciding the executive had to go. Afterwards the improvement in performance was amazing. Life at the top is not easy when difficult decisions have to be made.

In the case of the company using *Change with,* discussed earlier in this chapter, there was a very specific crucial enabling factor. It was the courageous managerial decision to take their best development engineer out of a revenue-earning role to concentrate on implementing a new design and order handling computer programme. This was essential for the organisational changes to work.

The rhetoric of change can be very persuasive yet very misleading. In one presentation on change I was, for my sins, carried away by the rhetoric. I waxed lyrical about how "We live in a world of continuous and increasing change. Everything is changing: what and how we think, the social fabric, the nuclear family, how we teach, how we relate, how we live, how we shop, what we can buy, how we spend our leisure time, how we work, how we organise. The wind of change has become the hurricane of change."[iii] Fine rhetoric and poetic words but I did over egg the pudding.

There have of course always been changes: some singularly cruel and disruptive such as those wrought by the agrarian and industrial revolutions. Each generation experiences changes of different kinds and magnitudes. Each generation thinks the changes it experiences are a dramatic break from the past. As Henry Mintzberg once asked, 'Why does every generation have to think that it lives in the period of greatest turbulence?'

Technology changes quickly but as discussed in Chapter 12, human nature changes remarkably slowly. Things change, people don't. Despite technology we are still basically like we always were and have not evolved at anything like the exponential rate of science and technology. There is a huge and continual mismatch between the two.

[iii] *Peter Moyes presentation* The Common Sense of Change *given at a Digital Portugal event*

However change is dressed up and whatever labels are used, the essence of *effective* change should be concerned with identifying the what, the why and the how:

a.   What changes are proposed?

b.   Why they are necessary?

c.   How will they be done?

Effective change means defining *purpose* before trying to change *process* and looking at the whole rather than the pieces. Those managing change need to:

1.   **Have a vision** - There is no better expression of vision than a carving on a gravestone in a Sussex dated 1730: 'A vision without a task is but a dream. A task without a dream is but drudgery. A vision and a task are the hope of the world'[iv].

2.   **Ensure there is focus** - Change frequently fails because there is no proper focus. One company I visited had no less than 12 change groups and incredibly wondered why they were not succeeding!

3.   **Make Changes Mind Sized** - Change can only be managed successfully if people at each level in the organisation can get their minds round it. People need to understand what it means to them.

[iv] *Quoted by Dr Sheila Sheinberg in her brilliant article <u>Managing Transformation</u> published in The Journal of Quality Management March 1991. JQM is published by Marian College, 45 South National Avenue, Fond Du Lac WI 54935, USA.*

4. **Utilise Wisdom -** Remember the importance of self-knowledge and wisdom and help people to know and trust themselves. Too often change fails because those sponsoring the change seriously underestimate the ability and worth of those who will be affected by the changes.

5. **Avoid Ubiquitous Solutions -** Avoid, like the plague, the illusion and false security of certainty: the ubiquitous answer, the ubiquitous methodology, the ubiquitous model, the ubiquitous solution or the ubiquitous theory. In the real world there are no final, permanent or finite answers or solutions only difficult choices and relevant questions.

6. **Remember Truth is Many-Sided -** Facts can be used to prove almost anything. Ultimately human beings believe what they want to believe. Effective change depends on perception.

7. **Avoid Bureaucracy -** I once saw a 27-page change questionnaire design to 'get the facts'. What nonsense! Beneficial changes are not promoted by idiotic questionnaires or by bureaucracy.

8. **Do What is Good -** Ensure that what is best is never the enemy of what is good. Some progress is better than no progress.

9. **Keep it Simple -** Paradoxically, although change is difficult and complex, effective change is

ultimately always simple (but not simplistic) in its implementation.

10. **Trust Intuition** - Analysis and logic are, at best, frail tools. There is no escaping the need to make intuitive and informed judgements.

11. **Go with the Energy** – Successful change needs energy.

Change is about working with human nature. Sensible architects (yes there are a few) know that the best way to design the layout of paths around new buildings is to grow grass first then put the paths where the grass is most worn. Sensible managers work with people wherever possible to see where their paths of energy are.

Effective change is as much or more about the heart as it is about the head and needs extraordinarily good people skills. It starts in the mind but it only works when there is vision, purpose, emotional buy-in and intellectual acceptance. What we do depends on what we *think*. How well be do it depends on what we *feel*. Successful change is about what happens in both heads and hearts.

This needs care, caution and compassion. Effective change needs integrity to do what is right and the intelligence to devise the right means of doing so. It needs understanding to recognise that change is about people, not things, and having the humility and common sense to act accordingly. This by any measure is a tall order but it is what is required to successfully initiate and manage change. In short, management at its best requiring the Wisdom of Solomon and the Patience of Job!

Chapter 14 - Cope with Crises

As you go through life, there are thousands of little forks in the road, and there are a few really big forks — those moments of reckoning, those moments of truth.
LEE IACOCCA

Management is a roller coaster. As in life, there are twists and turns and ups and downs. Nothing tests the mettle of a manager more than how he or she handles the down of a crisis 'the moment of truth', the 'moment of reckoning'.

Crises bring the best out of the good leader and the worst out of the bad manager. Some go to pieces, some contrive to ignore the reality and leave others to cope, some do too little too late. Others cope remarkably well and go from strength to strength and treat a crisis as an opportunity. How managerial leaders handle a major crisis is often the defining point for their careers and even of their organisation.

The ability to cope with a crisis is partly a matter of temperament and partly experience. "A smooth sea never made a skilful mariner[i]" and a manager who has lived in a protective bureaucratic environment is very likely to find it difficult to cope with a crisis. Whilst the mark of a fully rounded manager is the ability to cope with virtually anything, managers who excel in crisis situations and troubleshooting roles are not always the best managers in other situations.

---

[i] *Anonymous*

225

All managerial leaders will have, at one time or another, to cope with crisis situations. Some appear to manage in crisis mode all the time and if there isn't a crisis they invent one! Some crises are self-induced by delusions of grandeur, by over optimism (sometimes business related, sometimes technology initiated), by profligate expenditure, by lack of control, or simply by poor judgement that we all experience from time-to-time. Other crises are created by external events and hit a company like a bolt from the blue. Whatever the cause, real crises (as distinct from pretend crises) can never be ignored.

I joined Multitone Electric Co Ltd in 1974. Initially I was the Production Director but subsequently took over the design and development portfolio to become Technical Director. In the former role I was stunned to walk into a self-inflicted crisis when money was flowing out of the company as if it was going out of fashion. I was not sure then and I am not sure now, many years after the event, if my colleagues on the Board really understood how serious the situation was.

To add to my concerns, the design and reliability of many of Multitone's products left a lot to be desired. Proper quality assurance, as distinct from the pretend and bureaucratic paperwork variety, was in its infancy in the company. The production function was organised for mass production methods, which were wholly inappropriate for the company's customised 'to-order' market environment. Some of the methods were laughable. I was appalled by what I saw and had inherited. It really was a shambles.

Nor was it what I had been led to expect at interviews. Before joining the company I thought I had done my homework. I found out as much as I could, I questioned the key directors and went carefully through the published accounts for previous years. If, however, I had the sense to ask to see a copy of latest management accounts I would have doubtless seen how bad the balance sheet was. In the event, I was like a lamb going to slaughter and nothing prepared me for what I had inherited.

The origins of the crisis may have stemmed from the ambitions of the Managing Director who was able, energetic, charming and unfailingly courteous and seeking to expand the company. In doing so he tried to oversee the production and technical functions (and much else besides) in meticulous detail almost as his personal fiefdoms – or rather he did until I arrived.

I remember how astonished I was in my first week when he suggested I went to our Marham factory in Norfolk, England as otherwise, nothing would be produced. For someone like me from Philips, where factories almost worked in spite of management, this was a shock! Unfortunately what he said was true - but not for long! Management, in my book, is not about giving detailed instructions or spoon-feeding but about setting directions, enthusing people and giving them space to grow and learn from mistakes.

The perception I formed is that my predecessor (who I felt was the scapegoat) was that he was treated badly when he left despite my entreaties and protests. He had clearly done the MD's bidding and embarked on a plan to expand production much faster than sales and virtually without reference to the Commercial and Sales Director. Rightly or wrongly, I sensed that the MD had increased production capacity in an attempt to drive sales up. This is never a sensible thing to do and inevitably money was flowing out faster than money was coming in as production built up output, inventory and work-in-progress ahead of sales.

Fortunately for me, I inherited the nucleus of a really superb new production management team (Frank Brooks, Tony Headley, Duncan MacKay and George Ward) and subordinates they recruited or inherited. The team had to think and do the impossible. They had to be very tough with some of our suppliers including ones who had supplied the company for years. We stopped unnecessary supplies coming in and therefore money going out. We made already long payment periods even longer. We re-negotiated supply contracts (without incurring cost penalties) and then started the process of replacing unreliable suppliers.

Within weeks we had put in hand major changes in production methods, accelerated the introduction of effective quality assurance and started to address a host of technical problems and issues that had previously been ignored. In a whirlwind of activity, we were challenging the conventional wisdom of Multitone and consequently did not always win friends in doing so. In fact we sometimes rode rough shod over the old guard and that did not go down well at all.

Within a few months we started to see improvements slowly taking hold but it was two year before stocks were down to reasonable levels. It took even longer before the company was able to always pay staff a few working days before the end of the month instead of on the last day or at the beginning of the next month. The latter had hardly instilled confidence in staff.

The crisis was a turning point for Multitone because it accelerated long overdue changes and improvements. Successful crisis management should always force a company or organisation to address key problems it has ignored. Multitone was no exception.

The cash crisis was followed not long afterwards by a product crisis. There was an urgent need to rapidly re-design our first 'wide-area pager'. It was proving to be unreliable, particularly in regions such as Canada where static electricity was a problem. Our success in the re-design enabled Multitone to expand its foothold into the wide-area paging market at the expense of Motorola who had, to date, dominated the market. Production volumes increased dramatically this time to meet real orders. Thanks to the cash and profits generated, it paved the way for Multitone to later secure a stock exchange listing.

The success was not, of course, solely down to the dramatic improvements in the production and technical functions although this was the enabler. It owed much to the commercial director and to the delightful charm of the late Alex Polianakoff, the lovable if irascible chairman. Some years later I learned that a major reason why Multitone got its first large wide-area paging order from Bell was because of his charm. Being taken to lunch at the Savoy Hotel in the chairman's Rolls Royce greatly impressed their evaluation team. Such is the way of the world!

Crises change (even improve?) with the telling, particularly if the telling is many years after the event. They are a bit like being caught out by a storm in a boat. The experience is horrific but afterwards the perspective tends to become heroic. We forget the bad and remember only the good bits. Our minds also rationalise and dramatize the events in a crisis and they become war stories as this one has.

When a company or organisation is in the throes of a major setback or crisis its managers often have to cope with and adapt to a major change in circumstances, which is outside their comprehension and experience. The old certainties are replaced with distinctly uncomfortable new uncertainties. Managers feel threatened and insecure, as their collective experience and accumulated wisdom no longer seem relevant.

What people know they should do is not the same as what they actually do. In a crisis there is always a tendency, if not a compulsion, to act and pretend as though nothing has changed or needs to change. Institutions and the individuals in them, enter a state of denial as the Catholic Church did when confronted with irrefutable evidence of child abuse by priests.

The easy option is to ignore the bad news, hope for good news and in today's world put a spin on the events. This easy option is only a reaction to events rather than to try to make changes to prevent recurrence. The easy option is to follow not lead, to do too little too late and to muddle though and usually, watch the crisis deepen.

The danger for crisis-ridden managers is to yearn for the good old days. These are when sales and profits were growing at a handsome rate year in year out, when margins were high and the only problems were the congenial ones of managing growth and success. If only the golden age of bygone days would return. What nostalgic bliss: like those idyllic memories of childhood when the sun always seemed to shine in summer, when there was snow on Christmas day and when it hardly ever rained. Nothing is more comforting in a crisis, or more harmful, than the illusion of security and seeking certainty through the nostalgia of the past.

This happened to a small company I was once asked to help. It had enjoyed an Indian summer when its one major customer placed large orders for its one and only, over-priced and high margin product. The director-owners drove around in expensive BMW cars and did not have a care for what the future might bring. The Managing

Director, a born salesman, liked nothing more than wining and dining and would do so on any pretext even when the coffers were empty.

Inevitably, their customer learned sense and understood the true price of the product and took their business elsewhere. Instead of looking for new customers and markets the directors did nothing and pretended to themselves that all was well. They had meetings, kept the accounts, talked about what they had done and that was it, even thought they were in the most serious trouble.

At the moment of truth, when the need to respond to the new crisis situation can no longer be denied, as stated in the opening paragraph of this chapter, managers behave in different ways. Some are rational and some are irrational. Some behave well, some badly. Some are consistent and rational and some are inconsistent and irrational. Some clam up, some open up. When the Titanic was sinking, apparently the response of some of the crew was to re-arrange deck chairs and the band continued to play. How very tragic but also, how very human. In a crisis people cope, or fail to cope, in diverse and unpredictable ways.

People hold things back. They communicate part of their inner truths, they conceal part and they reveal parts that are the opposite of what they really think and feel. They deceive themselves. They worry about what their boss might think and do but keep their worries to themselves. They worry about their future and the threats (real or imaginary) to their position. In a crisis this process goes into overdrive and no one admits what he or she really thinks or feels.

When the chips are down a leader has to keep his or her head 'while everyone around is losing theirs.'[ii] A leader who is sucked into the black hole becomes part of the typical crisis cycle of frenetic activity punctuated by apathetic inactivity. He or she is doomed to failure.

Too often in crisis situations there is a lack of grip. This is particularly so in large organisations where there is little or no accountability and flat managerial structures. Boards or Senior Managers tend to set up umpteen working parties and committees discussing everything but deciding nothing. They almost get to the point where, if there were a fire, they would have a fractious meeting to decide whether to send for the fire brigade by first or second-class post! They also tend to make grandiose decisions that have no relevance to reality. Illusion displaces reality. There are rounds of long and inconsequential crisis meetings with inconclusive discussions and endless paralysis caused by endless analysis. Deadlines come and go. One priority is replaced with another priority. There are threats and ultimatums, depression, frustration and paranoia. Some are driven to tears, some to tantrums, and some to both. In short, people run round in circles like headless chickens.

Anyone who has lived through a crisis in a large organisation will instantly recognise this description. It is

---

[ii]   *Rudyard Kipling from the poem "IF"*

similar to what seems to have happened in IBM when the realisation first dawned that it faced a massive crisis. At one point the then Chief Executive was reported as having accused staff of spending too much time gossiping at the vending machines instead of getting out and selling. His remarks castigating his staff spread around IBM like a bush fire on their internal e-mail system and were quickly published worldwide. The CEO committed the cardinal sin in management and blamed others instead of blaming himself. There was no way he could survive after that. Even the idiotic generals in the First World War, far removed from the reality of the battlefront, did not publicly blame their troops, although some did so privately.

That particular CEO had been an excellent salesman and sales manager in the good times when the world was the oyster for IBM. Then the classic IBM sales tactic of account control and FUD (fear, uncertainty, doubt) was used to sell computers. Mainframe computers were hugely expensive and wrapped in awe and mystique. They were housed in special cathedral-like accommodation and only the high priests, the computer experts themselves, could gain access.

When the computers and the theology surrounding them changed, IBM failed to change. In such situations, effective managerial leaders know deep down that they and their organisations have to change in order to survive. They know they have to think the unthinkable and to metaphorically walk through a valley of the shadow of death to challenge and question cherished assumptions and beliefs. They know they have to learn to do new things in new ways and cope with an unfamiliar and unstable environment.

On the other hand, IBM continued with the maxim of 'business as usual'. With the advent of the mini-computer as a viable (and superior) alternative, their sales pitch ceased to work quite as well. They were now operating in a different league, but did not know it. Their customers became less-awed by computers and much less inclined to do what IBM said they should, nor were they as prepared to pay through the nose for the privilege.

The crisis at IBM only started to be resolved when Lou Gerstner was appointed Chief Executive and used classical command and control management (so despised by modern theorists) to rescue the company from itself. He did a really superb job in pulling IBM back from the brink. Almost all the armchair critics, experts and pundits criticised Gerstner for his centralised approach and for not dismembering and decentralising IBM. Gerstner was proved right and his critics were proved wrong.

The essential attributes of a leader in a crisis situation are a clear head, strong nerves and an iron determination not to be submerged by a rising mountain of papers, files, problems and decisions. The leader really has to rise above and be apart from the panic and apathy. The leader has to have imagination although too much can be distinctly unhelpful in a crisis. The leader has to be objective, determined and unswerving and to have an inner belief. The leader who cannot do these things becomes part of the problem and not part of the solution. The only option then is to help re-arrange the deck chairs on the sinking Titanic and enjoy the music from the band — while it lasts!

Despite the apparent complexity and daunting nature of a crisis, the actions needed to deal with it are surprisingly simple. A 'company doctor' once told me that what he essentially did, when he took over a crisis-ridden company, was to stop money going out (by placing firm controls on all expenditure and payments and by cutting costs) and increase money coming in (by chasing debtors, selling assets and increasing prices). He said that 70% to 80% of the time this was enough to save a company and could have been done without his involvement.

At one point in my career I helped to merge the loss making Ekco Avionics into MEL and transfer it from Southend-on-Sea, Essex to Crawley in Sussex. It was a particularly poignant experience for me as many years before I was trained for a week there on repairing Ekco TV.s. The first thing the Commercial Director of MEL did after the move was to increase prices by 10% and that largely solved the problems. I can still remember the wry comment of the Managing Director of Avionics "but if we have had done that we would not have needed to move or merge." He was right! Resolving a crisis is not rocket science.

For several years, I was a non-executive Director at Data

Recording Instruments, a public sector company with a chequered history. The Managing Director told me that when he took over he personally vetted and approved every payment and every item of expenditure. In a matter of months he made a significant impact on the ailing finances of the company and learned a great deal about what made it tick by these simple actions. Doing what he did was hard work but then who said management in a crisis is easy?

In a crisis the leader has to live through the anguish, jettison pet theories and deeply held beliefs, face the new reality as it is and test assumptions and proposals against that reality. The process is demanding but the success of living through it is infinitely rewarding. It can and does make or break a manager.

The worst way of facing a crisis is to bring in armies of consultants and gurus to advise what should be done. The last thing anyone needs in a crisis is the complexity, methodologies, models and theories of do-it-by-the-book mega fee consultants. There is never a shortage of them at the best of times. At the worst of times they are a real menace.

There are always hordes of would-be advisers who are only too eager to peddle and prescribe the latest fads, nostrums and panaceas. A bulky, indigestible and expensive report that recommends doing nothing and doing everything is useless. Life in a crisis is difficult enough without channelling effort and faltering energies in the wrong direction. When a ship is sinking the need is to pump water out not suck more in. This simple truth is often overlooked. (I used to sail and once heard of an instance where the bilge pump in a small boat was fitted the wrong way round and pumped water in instead of out!)

Crisis management needs a simple, clear and articulate analysis of what needs to be done, why, how, when and by whom. To formulate this requires insight, clarity, creativity, determination and originality. The key is pragmatism and gaining the right perspective. The need is to articulate an action plan, which is so clear, so simple and so practical that it is widely understood and accepted, emotionally and intellectually. Anything less is failure.

Above all else managers in a crisis need sufficient self-confidence to put their worries and fears aside. As President Theodore Roosevelt so perceptively remarked in the mid 1930's, when the US economy was in serious depression, 'all we have to fear is fear itself'. To banish the fear of fear, managers have to walk tall and use common sense to turn problems into opportunities. They have to appear calm and confident even though they may feel anything but confident or calm. Then the leader will '... be a man my son!'[iii] That is the true test of the mettle of an effective leader and the resilience needed to overcome a crisis.

[iii]   *Kipling ibid*

Chapter 15 - Provide Leadership

We can't all, and some of us don't. That's all there is to it.
— EEYORE - Winnie the Pooh by A A Milne

Providing leadership is the one thing that ultimately matters more than anything else in a successful organisation. Leadership is the innate ability to achieve, articulate, coordinate, drive, inspire, organise, motivate, get things done and think clearly in the ways described in chapters 8 to 14. The prime task of a leader is to make a beneficial difference. To do so is the hallmark of a leader.

A leader has, at one time or another, to be all things to all people. The attributes of a leader include being an advisor, analyst, catalyst, confidant, conceptualist, critic, devil's advocate, director, father figure, energiser, guru, innovator, judge, mother figure, organiser, practitioner, prophet, strategist, role model, synthesiser and much else besides. In the real world no one has such an extensive combination and range of life skills. Nevertheless, good leaders have more than a fair share and crucially make the fullest use of the ones they have. Determination, grit, persistence and resilience also go a long way. Robust health is a must in most cases.

This view may be an anathema to those who seek to classify leaders into categories such as Coercive Leaders, Authoritative Leaders, Affiliate Leaders, Democratic Leaders, Pace Setting Leaders and Coaching Leaders or whatever. As an academic exercise in classification or stamp collecting fine, but what does it contribute to making a beneficial difference in the real world? What matters, within the limits of decency, is what leaders *achieve* not their style of doing so.

Another approach used by academics, usually psychologists, is based on a kind of clone theory. The practitioners use psychological tests, such as Myers-Briggs, to measure and profile the kind of personality and other characteristics successful leaders have. The basic weakness of this approach is that the essence of leadership is diversity *not* conformity. I have met few successful managerial leaders who I would subjectively judge are out-and-out conformist. It is significant that few if any of the management hero role models are conformists. No one would accuse Bill Gates, Sir Richard Branson, Sir John Harvey-Jones, Sir Alan Sugar, Michael O'Leary the late Steve Jobs or Jack Welch as being conformist—anything but. Jack Welch in his autobiography makes it abundantly clear he is not a conformist. How could he be? Mavericks sometimes make very good leaders.

A further problem with the clone approach is the definition of success and the choice of who to clone. Who decides who the successful role models are? Are they the ones who are the best self-publicists because if they are then are the psychologists measuring skill at self-publicity? Are they ones academics think are successful because if so are the academics simply making self-fulfilling prophecies? Are they the rich and powerful or are the psychologists simply measuring the characteristics you need to become rich and powerful? The reality is that what makes for success is, like beauty, in the eye of the beholder.

At their best, profiling techniques may be reasonably good guides to personality types and incidentally they are fun to do, particularly at parties. In my experience all types of personalities succeed in leadership roles. In any case, there is far too much hidden subjectivity in the tests to rely on their conclusions.

There are also clearly limits to how accurate or inaccurate psychologists are in their assessments. As I was writing this there was a TV programme where psychologists assessed 1,000 applicants to determine who would be "ideal" marriage partners for each other. They identified only two couples with supposedly matching characteristics. The couples married without seeing their prospective partners beforehand. One marriage failed within three weeks. I would be loath to use psychologists to pick leaders!

Good leaders are recognisable by their performance but despite lots of theories there is little hard evidence about why and how they succeed. President Kennedy described leadership as 'one of the most observed and least understood phenomena on earth'. Some successful leaders are hands-off others are hands-on. Some drive by tasks, some drive by numbers, some use sticks, some use carrots. Some are highly visible and charismatic. Some are not. Some work quietly behind the scenes pulling the strings of power like a puppet master. Ultimately what matters is that they achieve positive outcomes and make a beneficial difference

There is no infallible way of determining if a would-be managerial leader has the particular or peculiar combination of skills that lead to success. It seems leadership is mainly a question of aptitude, as so many different kinds of people from diverse backgrounds succeed as managers. I have seen people succeed, as managerial leaders who I was sure would fail and people fail that I was certain would succeed. I have seen individuals perform brilliantly as a number 2 and fail abysmally as a number 1.

There seems no rhyme or reason as to what makes for success or failure in leadership. Some successful leaders are introverts some are extroverts. Some are academic. Some are not. Successful leaders have all kinds of backgrounds: accountancy, engineering, marketing, and sales. But background, like personality, is no guide to likely success. To make matters even more complex, one successful manager may use an approach and style almost diametrically opposed to that of another equally successful manager.

Sir John Harvey-Jones, who used to be Chief Executive of ICI, echoes this conclusion. He wrote 'I find myself intolerant of management books that seek to prescribe exactly 'how it should be done'. My own experience shows that there any many different ways of achieving one's aims. I have worked with leaders whose style is so totally different to my own that I have found it almost incomprehensible that they achieve results, but nevertheless they did. Each one of us has to develop our own style and our own approach, using such skills and personal qualities as we have inherited'.[i]

It is clear that all kinds and manner of people become successful leaders. Good leaders have aptitude and well-developed people skills. Leadership, like life, is something we learn the hard way in the university of life. It is not something we learn the easy way by reading a book or attending a training course or going to university or business school.

In some ways developing leadership attributes is like an apprenticeship. Mine started in my early teens when I was appointed a Patrol Leader in the 2nd Mirfield Boy Scouts when I organised my first patrol camp. It was a salutary leadership learning experience I will never forget. I had sole responsibility for the welfare of 5 younger children, it rained almost continually and there was wartime food rationing to contend with. Ensuring all members of the patrol kept warm, dry and happy was not easy. As I quickly learned, the real test of a leader is how well he or she copes in difficult circumstances. Some people have the right mix of life skills and can manage and lead. Others *don't* and *can't*.

This may seem black and white but time and time again, as

[i] *John Harvey-Jones Making it Happen – Reflections on Leadership (London: Fontana/Collins 1988) p26. ISBN 0-00-637409-3*

a manager and consultant, I have seen would-be managerial leaders fail simply because they did not have the aptitude, life skills or temperament. There is nothing wrong in this. All of us are good at some things and bad at others. We cannot all be good mathematicians, or musicians or stonemasons or whatever. We all have a collection of innate skills, which make us good at combinations of some things and weak at other combinations.

Intelligence is clearly important in any leader or manager but it is not the be all and end all by any manner of means. What matters perhaps more than IQ is EQ (emotional quotient) or practical intelligence. The latter is the innate ability to perceive what needs to be done and to understand how to get it done. Academic intelligence may be a mixed blessing in a leader.

Animal cunning is sometimes as important as or more important than intelligence. Only a foolish leader ignores the teachings of Niccolò Machiavelli[ii]. The truth is that people long on brains but short on experience and understanding of human nature are often disasters waiting to happen. When they do screw up they don't even realise they have done so.

Wisdom is a priceless life and managerial skill. A wise leader is worth his or her weight in gold. But what is wisdom and what is wise? The leader who seeks to

---

[ii] Niccolò Machiavelli *The Prince* (London: Penguin Classics 1981). *This is a "must read" and one of the few common sense textbooks on management.*

understand complexity while realising it is impossible to do so is wise. The wise leader welcomes those who *seek* the truth and but never those who know they have *found* the truth. The wise leader understands the difference between dependent and independent variables and does not make the mistake of trying to cure the symptoms instead of the cause. The wise leader never lets what is best become the enemy of what is good. The wise leader knows that what gets measured gets done and what gets praised gets done well[iii]. As to wisdom, well President Roosevelt defined it as "knowing what to do next."

The really wise leader gives all the credit for successes to his colleagues and subordinates and takes all the blame for all the failures. That is hard to do and takes most of us almost a working lifetime to learn but it truly is wisdom in action. As Lao Tzu put it 'A leader is best when people barely know he exists, when his work is done, his aim fulfilled, they will say: we did it ourselves'.

Wisdom comes in many guises and is not simply a function of a high IQ. Wisdom in organisational life does not always mean wisdom in personal life. I have known people who were wise in business who appeared to be singularly foolish in their personal lives. None of us are wise all the time in all situations and even the wisest of people make mistakes and poor judgements from time to time.

[iii] *Richard Wells. Management Today January 1996.*

Pragmatism is an important leadership life skill. There are no universal or immutable truths in leadership (or in life, despite the fanatics who would have us believe otherwise) only dilemmas, complexity, paradoxes and ever changing shades of grey. Managerial leadership is about coping with these. The pragmatic and practical leader always ensures that any course of action he or she embarks upon is clear, simple and practical. 'Keep it simple stupid' really is important for managerial success. Good leadership has always been about doing a few key simple things well. Is it clear? Is it simple? Will it work?

Intuitively knowing is an essential life skill. The good leader knows when something feels right or when a judgement is good (or bad). They may not be able explain why in analytical terms however. A lot of managerial leadership is about these kinds of soft and intangible life skills, which we rarely talk about. Good leaders have a sixth-sense based on knowing and wisdom. Deep down they know intuitively what to do. What distinguishes the effective leader from the ineffective is that the effective one trusts what he or she knows and acts on that trust.

The success of any organisation depends, as it always has done, on what the organisation does and how well it does it. The task of the leader is to decide, as it always has been, what an organisation or group should do and motivate the people in the organisation or group to do so. Outstanding leaders ensure that their organisations become outstandingly successful by doing the 'right' things, at the right time and doing them outstandingly well.

There is a key difference between management and leadership. Some years ago the Wall Street Journal carried a piece, which read: 'People don't want to be managed. They want to be led. Whoever heard of a world manager? World leader? Yes. Educational leader, political leader, religious leader, Scout leader, Labour leader and Business leader? Again, the answer is yes. They all lead, or they should do, they don't manage. The carrot always wins over the stick. Ask your horse. You can lead your horse to the water but you can't manage him to take a drink. If you want to manage somebody, manage yourself. Do that well and you'll be ready to stop managing and start leading'. Dated as it may be it is remarkably good sense.

One of the most sensible ways I know of making things happen is Action Centred Leadership[iv] (yes, I know it is a theory!). I first learned the value of this from the late John Garnett, Head of the Industrial Society and one of the most remarkable and charismatic individuals I have ever met. His action-orientation and his ability to stick to the essentials were awe inspiring and an inspiration to everyone who came into contract with him.

John Adair conceived action Centred Leadership[v] out of his experience in the army. It is based on the deceptively simple proposition that the effective leader balances the needs of diverse individuals within the team with the

---

[iv] *Leadership Training: A Report on the Application of Action-Centred Leadership (London: The Industrial Society 1970).*
[v] *John Adair The Action-Centred Leader (London: Industrial Society Press) ISBN 0-85290-460-6*

collective needs of the team as a whole and with the need to achieve the tasks that have to be done. Its simple mantra is the task, the team, the individual. As Adair put it himself, 'people need to know where they are going, literally or metaphorically, in terms of their common task. Secondly, they need to be held together as a team. Last but not least, each individual, by virtue of being human and personal, also brings a set of needs that require satisfaction'[vi].

ACTION CENTRED LEADERSHIP

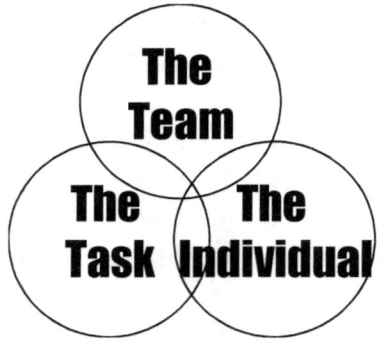

There are many in the politically correct and complicated world of management theory who will be sceptical of such a simple approach. Yet, what else is there other than people and what is managerial leadership and organisation about if it is not getting the best out of people? The success of any organisation has always depended on the creativity, effort, dedication and ingenuity of its people.

[vi] *John Adair Effective Leadership (London: Pan Books 1983)*

Managers with a tunnel vision who only focus on tasks fail because they neglect the needs of people and don't build a team. Managers who concentrate only on individuals develop a blinkered and idealistic view of human nature and are hurt when people let them down as they always do. Finally, managers who build teams, to the exclusion of everything else, build nothing. Effective leaders achieve by setting tasks, by motivating teams and by caring about people. In my experience of management I have seen nothing so natural or so effective as Action Centred Leadership.

Leadership is not an intellectual or theoretical exercise. It is not about understanding the meaning of life, or the nature of the universe. It is not an experiment to test the latest theory from fantasy-land, or a dress rehearsal for life. It is not about intellectual prowess. It is not about sitting at a computer for hours on end examining 'what if 'calculations on spreadsheets. Nor is it about surfing the Internet for useless information. Leadership *is* about real achievements made by real people in the real world. Leadership is about a 'can-do-will-do-now' approach not a 'can't-do-won't-do-wait-and-see' approach

Ultimately leadership really is a question of suck it and see. The ultimate test of any leader is does he or she succeed? As Robert Townsend[vii] said '…the true leader can be recognised because, somehow or other, his people

---

[vii] *Robert Townsend Up The Organization – How to stop the company stifling people and strangling profits (London: Coronet Books 1971) ISBN 0 340 14986 8 p90.*

consistently turn in superior performances'. The only way to find out is to try them. Some have a natural leadership aptitude and life skills, some don't. The world of management would be much healthier if instead of trying to select leaders according to some theoretical criteria we backed those who have the life skills to succeed.

The danger is that leadership is becoming a lost art. 'Most hierarchies are nowadays so cumbered with rules and traditions, and so bound in by public laws, that even high employees do not have to lead anyone anywhere, in the sense of pointing out the direction and setting the pace. They simply follow precedents, obey regulations, and move at the head of the crowd. Such leaders do so only in the sense that the carved wooden figurehead leads the ship.'[viii] This eloquently sums up why organisations need *real* managerial leadership.

[viii] *Peter and Hull The Peter Principle*

Chapter 16 – Build Cathedrals

Fear not the path of truth because of the lack of people walking on it.
— ARAB PROVERB

Really successful organisations, like the stonemason in chapter 12, have a cathedral building culture and mentality. They know that their success, like that of any organisation or enterprise, depends on what the people in it do, how well they do it and on how well they are motivated. They realise that faith can move mountains, money never can and neither can theories.

Too many organisations make minimal use of intelligence and puzzle over their failures. Cathedral building managerial leaders make maximum use of intelligence and human ingenuity. They know employees want to grow and need to grow. To do so they give them real responsibility to take risks, learn from experience, make and acknowledge mistakes, stimulate curiosity, develop an inquisitive cast of mind, walk tall and expand their knowledge. They work from trust, not distrust. They use praise not criticism.

Organisations that build cathedrals treat people as human beings not machines. They eschew the machine like approach as a throw back from the absurdities of the so-called scientific school of management so beloved by Comrade Lenin. They know, as a middle-aged appliance worker once told Jack Welch, "For 25 years you've paid for my hands when you could have had my brain as well – for nothing."

251

For cathedral builders, organising people in co-operative groups or teams with clear objectives is the way to build a competitive and successful organisation in any culture in any part of the world. The mantra of Action Centred Leadership — the task, the team, the individual —is part of their organisational DNA.

To them, management is also inseparable from leadership. Without leadership, and the impetus, passion and vision leaders provide, there is nothing. 'When there is no vision, the people perish'.[i] Organisations decay unless they have leaders to provide belief, confidence and direction.

Cathedral Builders know leaders are not infallible and inevitably make mistakes. They know success is about admitting to and learning from mistakes. Leaders who fail try to hide their mistakes and don't learn from them.

They are also realistic about people and human nature. They understand that human actions can be modified to some extent but human nature cannot be changed. Organisations have to get the best out of people as they are, warts and all, and not what they would ideally like them to be. They know utopian fantasies don't work.

Human beings can be incredibly stupid or incredibly bright and sometimes both at the same time. Leadership is about fostering the bright and discouraging the stupid. Some highly intelligent people are sometimes very stupid when dealing with practical matters and can be extremely foolish. We all know highly intelligent people who cannot

---

[i] Proverbs xxxix 18

be let loose without a minder. That is why management is about matching horses for courses and using intelligence wisely.

Organisations produced by analysis and run on analysis fail because of 'paralysis by analysis'. Machines are the templates for analytical organisations. But people are neither machines nor machine like and organisations comprising people are of necessity complex organic entities. Organisations can never be reduced to pure analysis or theory nor can they be replaced by mechanistic intelligence even if hyped as artificial.

Effective managerial leadership is about action and getting things done. The common sense way of making things happen, of building cathedrals, is "keep it simple stupid" (KISS) and to not make the mistake of confusing simple with simplistic.

We suffer in management, as in society, from a kind of collective madness. This makes otherwise intelligent and sane people worship at the altar of unnecessary and mindless complexity and create even more complications. The truth is that simple things work and work well, whereas complex things are not robust and therefore more often than not fail.

Management is not about understanding complexity (which is almost certainly impossible) or dwelling on theoretical minutiae. Those are tasks for academia. Instead, it is about using common sense, intelligence, experience and wisdom to manage and succeed in spite of unfathomable complexities. Whereas theorists dwell on and dissect complexities, managers cope with them, manage around them or simply manage in spite of them. The wearer of a watch does not have to understand how its intricate mechanisms work to tell the time.

The ultimate complexity is the human being; all other complexities pale in comparison. President Kennedy (or, more probably, one of his speech writers) was wrong when he claimed 'space was the last frontier'. The human mind is the last and insurmountable frontier.

It is blindingly obvious to cathedral builders that:

- **Technologies are only a means to an end.** 'Computers can figure out all kinds of problems, except the things in the world that just don't add up.'[ii] That is what managers are for.
- **It is better to swim with the tide of events than against the tide.** Doing so is much more productive and successful although it is sometimes better to go even further and shape events.
- **Wise managers give all the credit for success to their subordinates.** They take personal responsibility for all the mistakes and failure. Doing so is hard. Praise is more effective than criticism – a lesson all leaders need to learn and re-learn by heart.
- **Pretend and synthetic knowledge are no use to anyone.** Management is not about the mindless accumulation of mindless information and the mindless labelling of it as knowledge. That is the

[ii] James Magary. Source not traced

task of one-storey thinkers not of managerial three-storey thinkers.

- **Management is dynamic.** There are never any definite, final or static answers in management. The managerial leader's job is to ask the right questions so that others will find and implement answers that are sufficient for the moment.

- **Management techniques are panaceas business schools believe managers should use but don't.** Wise managers selectively use a small number of the techniques and realise they are merely tools. Management and leadership cannot be reduced to technique (or theory) and there are no panaceas in either management or life.

- **The attempts to dress up management theories in pseudo scientific clothes are nonsense**. Whereas scientific theories can at least be subject to the proof of falsification and the lesser proof of experimental verification the vast majority of management theories are opinions presented as intellectual constructs. The scope for charlatans and woolly-minded thinkers is unfortunately immense in the Management Myth Making Industry. They do great harm.

- **An ounce of experience is worth a ton of theory.** Common sense, experience and wisdom are what really matter in management — and in most other things in life. Samuel Taylor Coleridge (1782-1834) believed that 'Common sense in an un-common degree is what the world calls wisdom'. In the Bible it says: 'Wisdom is the principal thing: therefore get wisdom; and with all thy getting get understanding.'[iii]

- **Great leaders and great strategists have always enunciated wisdom with elegant simplicity and incisive clarity.** That really is wisdom and should be the aspiration of all leaders. It is the real work of management. Managers succeed most when their objectives are Clear, Simple and Practical.

- **Decisions and tasks must be one-mind sized.** A manager must be able to get his mind round what he or she confronts. Any thing less is failure.

- **Minds are like umbrellas and only work when they are open**. Closed minds are the antithesis of successful management.

- **Management is multi dimensional.** In the short term a manager has to ensure his or her organisation *survives* and has often to react decisively to do so. In the longer term an organisation can only survive if it *thrives* otherwise it decays. That needs innovation, a proactive approach, self-discipline, an inner confidence and the introspective, self doubt upon which inner confidence is built.

- **One of the key determinants in management, as in politics, is "events, dear boy, events**[iv]. Managers and their organisations, no matter how successful, cannot walk on water. Sooner or later events or technology intrude and bite back. Wise managers always entertain the possibility that the light at the

---

[iii] Proverbs 4:7
[iv] Harold Macmillan when Prime Minister of the UK

end of the tunnel is an express train coming towards them.

There is no magic about management. Magic, if it exists at all, exists in people but this has not stopped us searching for magic or stopped peddlers of management snake oil from claiming they have found magic with their latest theories.

We are too often like the Lion in *The Wizard of Oz* who sought the magic of courage, the Scarecrow who sought the magic of a brain and Tin Woodman who sought the magic of a heart. They still wanted them even after they had discovered that the Wizard of Oz was a humbug. But then, as the Wizard of Oz explained, "How can I help being a humbug when all these people make me do things they know cannot be done?"[v] Quite so!

Fortunately, Oz was a kindly humbug with a shrewd understanding of "human" nature. He "solved" their problems by providing a drink of courage for the Lion, a brain of bran, pins and needles for the Scarecrow and a heart stuffed with sawdust for Tin Woodman. They then all lived happily ever after as they always do in fairy stories.

In management we can't live happily ever after although there are many Wizards, Gurus and Consultants who want us to believe we can. That is of course provided we pay them large fees for them to solve *our* problems with *their* nostrums, *their* prescriptions and *their* theories. They offer

---

[v] L Frank Baum *The Wizard of Oz* Chapter 16 p125

a supposedly comfortable, albeit expensive, illusion that can only lead to tears and disillusion.

Managerial Leaders, if they are to succeed and remain true to themselves, need to do what the Lion, Scarecrow and Woodman failed to do. They need to confront their illusions, throw away the props, ignore the Witch doctors and Wizards and lead from the front.

We have an abundance of knowledge, technology and information in modern society but not an abundance of insight and wisdom to use them effectively. So we need, above all else in management and society, to develop and cherish wisdom and experience. It is incredibly good sense to 'Believe nothing, no matter where you read it, or who said it, no matter if I have said it, unless it agrees with your own reason and you own common sense'.[vi] There is no better or more relevant advice for the successful practice of management and building cathedrals. What more is there to say?

END

[vi] This is sometimes credited to the Buddha but it is probably unlikely. If the Buddha did not say it he should have done!

Appendix

These are my top ten books on management, or relevant to management, arranged in alphabetical order of authors' name.

Russell L Ackoff – *The Art of Problem Solving*

This book is the result of thirty years' experience and it shows. Its advice is excellent and realistic. It is also free of hype and refreshingly humorous (too many books on management are written by serious middle aged men whose only future is to become serious old men!).

J A C Brown - *The Social Psychology of Industry*

This rare book really does nail the fiction that human beings can be regarded as machines or as isolated individuals. Its insights are remarkably good. It is particularly good on how informal organisations work and why and how autocrats create organisations.

Dale Carnegie – *How to Win Friends and Influence People*

Some think this book passé because it is folksy and they are dismissive of it because it is part of the self-improvement genre. But it is packed with the rare qualities of common sense and wisdom. It talks remarkably good sense about people and human nature. Many others obviously agree because it is still in print and a best seller more than sixty years after it was first published.

Peter F Drucker - *The Practice of Management*

This is the book almost all managers of my vintage were brought up on. It is a classic, brilliant, and seminal and an outstanding contribution to management. It is packed with insight, innate good sense and wisdom. His later books are also excellent.

Antony Jay – *Management and Machiavelli*

The author's ideas, breadth of vision, perception, presentational skills and realism are brilliant. Few other books on management come close. One of the most thought provoking and realistic books I have ever read.

Jeffrey Pfeffer and Robert I Sutton – *The Knowing-Doing Gap*

Although I am critical of this book for its failure to reach a conclusion and grasp the nettle, it addresses what in many ways is the central problem in management. It is packed with useful information. It is also mostly pragmatic and doesn't plug a favourite theory.

Thomas J Peters and Robert H Waterman Jr - *In Search of Excellence*

If you have never read this book do so. It was deservedly a run-away success.

Karl Popper – *The Open Society and its Enemies*

Although not a book on management, Adair Turner, a Director-General of the Confederation of British Industry, said this was the book that had influenced him most. I share his enthusiasm and his view that it "is the classic statement of a humane liberal and democratic philosophy". Popper's condemnation of the dangers of utopian social engineering is as relevant to management as it is to the body politic and is utterly persuasive. A difficult read but well worth the effort.

John Ralston Saul – *Voltaire's Bastards*

Another book, not about management, but having so much to say that is relevant to thoughtful managers. It is unique in its range and scholarship and is a devastating critique of our political, economic and culture establishments. Like Popper it is difficult to read and absorb but it is hugely stimulating.

Robert Townsend – *Up the Organization*

Robert Townsend's ability to express essential truths with elegant simplicity and incisive clarity is truly amazing. He has a rare and enviable gift as a writer. It leaves most books, including mine, in the shade. It is packed with practical advice and good sense based on experience of leading a successful organisation. Few successful managers write books. Even fewer academics write ones as brilliant.

And finally…

An Ant's Guide to Management Theory - YouTube

I'd like to add this to the above list, albeit it is a somewhat different offering. This 3-minute piece uses pictures rather than words – and a little bit of that all-important management commodity, humour, to get its point over. If you've come this far with me, I think you'll like it. It is of course only available via your PC, Laptop or Smartphone. Go to YouTube, add the above title in the YouTube 'search' option, then hit play, sit back and enjoy!

Appendix and Notes

Fantasy or Reality?

Appendix and Notes

Fantasy or Reality?